MW01040417

# The New Prepper's

# Water Survival Bible

## MARK RIVERS

**ISBN: 9798863574943**

10 9 8 7 6 5 4 3 2 1

# GET YOUR BOOK NOW!

Greetings and welcome! It's an honor to be speaking to the best audience in the world. I'm thrilled that you choose my "The New Prepper's Water Survival Bible.". I wanted to take a moment to thank you for your trust in me, I'd like to gift you another one of my books, the "Prepper's Survival Bible," a wonderful tool for anyone that want to learn tricks and secrets of the survival world, as a sign of my appreciation. To download it, simply follow the instructions below.

Again, thank you for your support, and I sincerely hope that both of these publications will assist you in realizing all of your culinary aspirations.

**To Download your book, scan the QR code below!**

You don't need to enter any personal details.

# Table of Contents

INTRODUCTION    6

CHAPTER 1    9

HARVESTING TECHNIQUES    9
Understanding the Nuances of Water Sourcing    9
DIY Harvesting Innovations    13

CHAPTER 2    21

FILTRATION FUNDAMENTALS    21
Diving into Filtration Systems    21

CHAPTER 3    32

PURIFICATION MASTERY    32
Chemical Purification Demystified    32

CHAPTER 4    47

EFFICIENT STORAGE SOLUTIONS    47
Selecting Appropriate Containers    47
Space-Saving Techniques    49

CHAPTER 5    54

INTEGRATION AND TACTICAL APPROACHES    54
Crafting Your Holistic Off-Grid Hydration Plan    54
Real-Life Case Studies    59

CHAPTER 6    66

BASIC DIY PLUMBING IDEAS    66
Plumbing Essentials for Off-Grid Living    66

CHAPTER 7    68

WATER SUSTAINABILITY    68
The Sustainable Water Paradigm    68

**CHAPTER 8**     **73**

FINDING WATER     73

  Mastering the Art of Water Discovery     73

CONCLUSION     78

# Introduction

The elixir of life, water, is something that most of us take for granted until it suddenly becomes scarce. It's easy to take this vital liquid for granted in a society where it only takes a second to get it by turning on a faucet. The supply of clean water is not a given, however, as history and nature have often shown us. Here, the need of learning to stay hydrated and alive without access to running water becomes apparent.

Envision a world where your reliable supply of water is abruptly cut off. Water supply disruptions can occur for a variety of reasons, including natural catastrophes, infrastructure breakdowns, and the unexpected. Having the know-how and supplies to obtain water on your own can save your life in such a crisis.

"Off-grid hydration" may sound like a side issue, but it's actually crucial to self-sufficiency and emergency planning. It's taking charge of one's own hydration needs instead of expecting others to provide for them.

The practice of finding, cleaning, storing, and saving water away from a central water supply is known as "off-grid hydration." To survive in the face of a shortage of potable water, you need a multifaceted plan that incorporates a wide range of theoretical understanding and hands-on expertise.

Mastering the complex terrain of water survival is analogous to mastering a wide range of skills, and it's an essential part of being self-reliant and disaster-ready. Preparation for the many obstacles and factors to be taken into account along this path is essential.

The first step in ensuring water security is finding a reliable supply. Several natural resources are available for water harvesting. To ensure a steady supply, it's critical to understand these origins. One of the most common techniques is collecting rainwater from roofs and other rooftops. Condensation traps can be a lifesaver in extremely dry climates. Groundwater can be reliably accessed by digging deeper reservoirs. Using these methods, you may take charge of your water security and live off the grid.

Once water is obtained, the next obstacle is making sure it is safe to drink. Microorganisms and chemical pollutants alike are common in natural water sources. You can protect yourself from waterborne diseases by using filtration and purification methods. There is a wide range of options available, from inexpensive cloth filters to high-tech UV purifying systems. The best way to ensure consistent water quality is to be familiar with these tools and know when to use them.

Having access to clean water is only half the battle. Implementing reliable storage methods is just as critical. If you ignore this, your water supply could deteriorate, rendering your efforts useless. Packaging, storage, and rotation methods all play a significant role at this stage. There should be a rotation system in place to make sure the oldest water gets utilized first, as well as the usage of containers that prevent contamination and deterioration. These actions are crucial to ensuring water availability in the future.

To survive without water, you need to do more than just find it, clean it up, and store it for the future. Knowledge of adjacent water sources, such as streams, lakes, or aquifers, can be lifesaving in a survival situation. Furthermore, being able to cleanse these impromptu water sources is a lifesaving ability in times of emergency. Knowing how to adapt to and make use of your environment in order to get water can be the difference between life and death whether camping in the outdoors or during a natural disaster.

Learn everything you need to know about water in the wild: where to get it, how to purify it, how to store it, and what to do in case of an emergency. All of these parts work together to produce a solid system that will keep you independent even if your regular water supply suddenly runs out.

Taking steps toward self-sufficiency benefits not just your own security, but also that of your neighbors and the larger community. As the essential elixir of life, water is crucial to our survival. You can help build a more resilient and prepared society, one drop at a time, by adopting preventative measures to protect your water supply.

# Chapter 1

# Harvesting Techniques

## Understanding the Nuances of Water Sourcing

### Recognizing Viable Water Sources in Different Environments

The availability of water is the single most important consideration for off-grid water survival. Anyone who want to achieve mastery in the skills of off-grid living and preparing is required to learn how to recognize and make use of trustworthy water sources in a range of different environments. In this in-depth examination, we examine the complexities of water sourcing, revealing the different sorts of water sources and the ways that are employed to protect this vital commodity. Water is a crucial resource, and its protection is of the utmost importance.

**Taking Advantage of the Rain to Collect Water:**

Collecting rainwater and putting it away for later use is a typical activity in regions that experience a high frequency of rainfall events. The process involves collecting rainwater as it falls and directing it into reservoirs so that it can be used at a later time. One of the benefits is a more consistent supply of water, and another is less pressure on non-traditional sources of supply. Rainwater is an excellent source of water due to the natural purity that it possesses. However, contamination can be avoided by collecting and preserving the specimens with extreme care.

Because of the scant amount of rainfall that occurs in arid locations, collecting rainwater can be an increasingly challenging endeavor. The use of rainwater catchment systems and fog nets are two examples of innovative water conservation measures that might be put into practice in a scenario such as this one. You will only be able to survive in the long run if you are able to make the most of the rain when it does finally arrive.

**Equipment for the Collection of Water:**

Condensation traps are a blessing in places like coastal regions and tropical rainforests, where the humidity levels and temperature changes are high. When warm, humid air is cooled to the degree where condensation can occur, condensation occurs. The water droplets that develop as a result of condensation can then be collected. Even while condensation traps do not produce a large volume of water at once, they can nevertheless be relied upon as a dependable source of potable water.

The same principle applies in dry environments, where it might be challenging to create the conditions necessary for condensation to occur. For example, solar stills make use of the temperature difference caused by the sun to evaporate soil moisture, which is then collected on a surface within the still where it condenses. It's possible that this strategy will be absolutely necessary to your survival in the worst of situations.

**The phrase "groundwater":**

Extracting groundwater has been a useful practice for a significant number of years. In areas with high water tables, such as in close proximity to rivers or lakes, the water that comes from a well may be reliable and steady. Wells can range from straightforward holes dug by hand to more involved boreholes that require drilling, depending on the requirements and the resources that are available.

Groundwater is an excellent source of clean drinking water since it is frequently found below the amount of contamination that is brought in from the surface. However, in order to prevent gradual pollution over time, wells need to be constructed and maintained in the correct manner. Researching the geology and hydrology of the area is another way to figure out where the best location is for drilling a well.

**Wetland Locations:**

The majority of ecosystems contain a variety of surface water sources, the most frequent of which are streams, rivers, and lakes. The availability of these commodities is crucial in both urban and rural settings. The pollution of these systems by human and animal waste as well as the presence of waterborne pathogens are only two examples of the unique challenges that are associated with the use of these systems.

Before it can be used appropriately, water drawn from the surface needs to go through the processes of filtering and purification. Purification methods like as boiling, chemical treatment, or UV sterilization eliminate pathogens and contaminants, while filtration removes bigger particles than other purification methods. It is essential to have the knowledge necessary to evaluate the water's quality in order to choose an appropriate treatment method before the water can be considered safe for human consumption.

**In Case of a Critical Situation:**

When there is a crisis, it is extremely crucial to know where and how to collect water because prepared supplies may run out or be disturbed in some other way. Knowing where and how to access water is especially important. In predicaments involving survival in the great outdoors or in the aftermath of a natural disaster, this is of the utmost importance.

In order to locate a water source, you should look for animal tracks that converge or for plants that are thriving. It is possible to reach groundwater by excavating a small hole in an otherwise dry riverbed or at the base of a hill. Collect the plant moisture, such as dew, that occurs in the morning. Although they may only give a limited amount, these methods have the potential to make the difference between living and dying in a desert.

**Desalination is the process of:**

People who live on or near the shore may find that desalination is a game-changer for their water supply. Desalination processes remove salt and other impurities from seawater, thereby making the water suitable for consumption. This is often performed by the utilization of distillation, reverse osmosis, or solar desalination processes. A renewable supply of freshwater in regions where the typical sources are salty, despite the fact that the procedures involved can be energy-intensive and require specialized apparatus.

## Surveying Essential Tools for Effective Water Collection

Water is necessary for life, and in today's contemporary society, we have easy access to it through the faucets in our homes. Because of the need for independence, the desire to plan for contingencies, or the desire to live off the grid, this convenience of access is not always available. Those who want to be self-sufficient in terms of water need to be able to obtain water in a variety of settings and also need to have the tools to collect, filter, and purify the water that they do find. In this comprehensive investigation, we will delve into the nitty-gritty of water sources and examine the key devices and implements that are required for effective water collecting. We will go through the foundations of off-grid hydration and survival, such as where and how to acquire water, how to store it, and how to get rid of contaminants after they have contaminated it.

### The Significance of Having Access to Water

The acquisition of a steady supply of water is the initial step in achieving self-sufficiency and being prepared for emergencies. In most situations, we tend to take the availability of clean water for granted; nevertheless, this is not always the case. In the first part of our research, we address the significance of water supply and delve into the complexities of off-grid hydration. This will be followed by an examination of the nuances of hydration.

We frequently fail to accord water, also known as the "elixir of life," the respect it merits despite the fact that it is absolutely necessary to our existence. When we turn on the sink faucet, water immediately begins to pour into our homes. This luxury of the 21st century is, however, susceptible to disruption, and we may be forced to face an uncomfortable truth: we are the ones who need to be responsible for ensuring our own water security. Finding a dependable source of water should be your number one objective if you have any interest in off-grid living, being better prepared for emergencies, or even just becoming more self-sufficient.

### A Present from Mother Nature, the Ability to Collect Water from the Clouds

We might be able to reduce our reliance on the water systems provided by the municipality if we harvested rainwater and stored it. This discusses the methods and tools required to collect rainwater as well as their respective benefits. Rain barrels, gutters, downspouts, and roof collection surfaces all play a significant role in the collection of precipitation in their respective environments. In addition, we talk about the advantages of collecting rainwater as well as the specifics that need to be considered.

### Making Use of Condensation Traps in Order to Collect Dew and Dew Drops from the Air

In conditions of low temperature and high humidity, the use of condensation traps can be of great assistance. They make it possible to capture atmospheric moisture even in locations that are wet or arid, and they can also do so along the coast. Details are provided for essential methods of survivability, including as solar stills and the modification of condensation traps for arid environments.

### Investigation of Underground Aquifers in Search of Unutilized Resources

Groundwater is a valuable resource that is located beneath the surface of the earth. Wells are a tried-and-true method for acquiring access to groundwater. The ins and outs of groundwater sourcing, such as the many types of wells and the best practices for ensuring the quality and safety of well water, are discussed in detail.

**Lakes, rivers, and streams are the types of waterways that are considered surface waterways.**

In a great number of habitats, there is a plethora of accessible surface water sources. However, they also come with their own unique set of challenges, such as the threat of contamination and the existence of diseases that are transmitted by water. We study the necessity of recognizing the availability of surface water, as well as the significance of filtration and purification in surface water source. In addition, we look at the significance of recognizing the availability of surface water.

### The Best Places to Search for Water During a Dry Period

It is necessary to be familiar with one's nearby area in order to find water during times of emergency or to survive. In this section, techniques for water survival, as well as the delicate balance that must be maintained between amount and quality, are described, along with the skill of locating sources of emergency water.

### Desalination: Making Possible What Was Once Thought to Be Impossible

Desalination offers an alternative in coastal regions where the high levels of salt in the groundwater make it difficult to rely on freshwater sources. We look into the many methods for desalinizing seawater and talk about the benefits and drawbacks of each one.

### Receptacles for the Golden Fluid that serve as Storage

Once a dependable source of water has been located, the next step is to collect it and put it away for use at a later time. The subject of this section is the collection containers, which are extremely important to the overall process that will be described. It has been suggested that several types of containers, including jugs, bottles, foldable containers, rain barrels, jerry cans, water bladders, and solar still bags, could be used to store water.

### Filtration Strategies for the Purification of the Crop

At first glance, there are some water sources that appear to be clean; nonetheless, it is critical to filter out any toxins before consuming the water. In this section, we'll investigate different filters that can be of use in dealing with that. There are several different approaches to filtering water, including those that may be used on the go, such as portable water filters, pump filters, gravity filters, and syringe filters. These approaches are discussed in detail.

# DIY Harvesting Innovations

## Constructing Improvised Water Gathering Devices

You should always be prepared for the possibility that you will need to collect water from nontraditional sources, as water is one of the most crucial elements for existence. A competence in constructing makeshift water gathering equipment can be invaluable in times of crisis, on outdoor expeditions, or in places where pure water is scarce. In this quick tutorial, we'll discuss some creative do-it-yourself methods for obtaining water from unconventional places.

**Silent Sun:**

Even in dry climates, clean water can be extracted from the ground using a solar still. A rock, a container, a digging tool, and a transparent plastic sheet are all you need to get started.

Steps:

- The first step is to dig a hole large enough to accommodate your container.
- To speed up the evaporation process, surround the container with wet plants or urine.
- Seal the opening with a transparent plastic sheet.
- Above the container, in the middle of the plastic sheet, place a tiny rock.
- Sunlight causes water to evaporate from the ground, condense on the plastic, and eventually trickle into the storage container.

**The Gathering of Rainwater:**

Water can be easily harvested by simply collecting rainwater. If you don't have a large enough container, a roof, or tarp, you'll need to improvise a funnel.

Steps:

- Put the container in the desired location for rainwater collection.
- The tarp or roof should be positioned over the container so that rainwater may be collected.
- Water can be channeled into the container by using a gutter or a homemade funnel made of plastic or other materials.

**Bags to Catch Exhaled Air:**

Plants exude water that can be collected for use in a survival crisis. This strategy is ideal for use in sunny, hot settings. Gather together a string, a green branch, and a transparent plastic bag.

Steps:

- Look for a green, leafy branch.

- The branch should be encased in the plastic bag.

- Make sure to leave a hole in the bag when you tie it around the branch.

- To dry the bag faster, hang it outside.

- The condensation produced by the leaves' exposure to the sun will fall to the bottom of the bag.

**Moisture Harvesting:**

In humid climates, dew can be a significant water source. An absorbent cloth or similar item is required.

Steps:

- Spread the fabric out on the ground, ideally in a dark spot where you can see the stars.

- Do not touch it until morning. In order to collect the dew, wring out the cloth in the morning.

**Point Well:**

It is possible to dig a well to reach groundwater in areas with sandy or loose soil. A pipe or tube, a shovel, and a storage unit are required.

Steps:

- Create a hole that goes below the water level.

- Put the pipe or tube into the opening.

- Cover the opening of the tube with a container.

- The tube will eventually become filled with groundwater from the surrounding area.

In a number of survival scenarios, improvised water collection systems are essential. These do-it-yourself methods can be used to gather water in arid, forested, or urban settings. Always cleanse water before drinking it to make sure it is safe to drink, as the quality of water you find can vary. When gathering water from the wild, it's important to adhere to any rules or laws that may be in place and to keep the environment in mind.

## Adapting Common Items for On-the-Spot Water Collection

It is important to be able to collect water in an emergency situation without any sophisticated tools. Luckily, with enough ingenuity and improvisation, you can use everyday items to find sources of water. In this detailed tutorial, you'll learn how to collect water from several sources, including the environment and common household items.

## 1. Plastic containers:

Plastic water bottles are convenient because they may be used for a variety of purposes and can be found almost anywhere. Some potential modifications are listed below:

A. Water Harvesting from Rain:

Bottles of plastic, a bladed tool (such a knife or scissors), and duct tape (but not required).

Steps:

- Make a funnel by slicing off the top of a plastic bottle.
- Turn the funnel upside down and insert it into the bottle's neck.
- Duct tape (not required) can be used to secure the joint.
- Put the bottle in a dripping faucet or next to a running faucet to fill up from rain.

B. Solar Steadfast:

Bottle of plastic, transparent plastic sheet or bag, shovel, storage container, and tape (if desired).

Steps:

- Create a water well by excavating a hole.
- Make sure your container is centered in the opening.
- To speed up the evaporation process, surround the container with wet plants or urine.
- Make a funnel by slicing off the top of the plastic bottle.
- Turn the funnel upside down and secure it to the bottle's opening.
- Seal the hole with a clear plastic bag or sheet, making sure it is airtight by filling it with rocks or dirt.
- In the middle of the plastic sheet, place the bottle with the funnel pointing down.
- Sunlight causes water to evaporate from the ground, condense on the plastic, and eventually trickle into the storage container.

## 2. textiles and apparel:

Dew collection, an approach particularly effective in humid areas, can be accomplished with clothing and fabric objects. This is how:

An Accumulation of Dew:

You'll need an absorbent cloth or fabric (like an old T-shirt) to get the job done.

Steps:

- Spread the fabric out in the open where it can have a good look at the stars.

- Do not touch it until morning.

- In order to collect the dew, wring out the cloth in the morning.

**3. Plastic Bags:**

Plastic bags are convenient for improvised water collecting because of their portability and light weight. How to use them is as follows:

A. Bag for Expiration:

You'll need a transparent plastic bag, a green branch, and some twine.

Steps:

- Look for a green, leafy branch.

- The branch should be encased in the plastic bag.

- Make sure to leave a hole in the bag when you tie it around the branch.

- To dry the bag faster, hang it outside.

- The condensation produced by the leaves' exposure to the sun will fall to the bottom of the bag.

B. Condensation bag:

You'll need a plastic bag, some small rocks or pebbles, some greenery, and some water.

Steps:

- Stuff the plastic bag with wet leaves or other plant matter.

- Create pits in the bag by placing a few stones or small rocks inside.

- You should secure the bag with a knot.

- To dry the bag faster, hang it outside.

- Condensation will build on the inner surface and gather in the depressions as the contents heat up and release moisture.

**4. Garments and Headgear:**

In a survival emergency, you can use your clothing and hat to catch rainwater. This is how:

A. Perspiration in Your Cap:

Supplies: Any type of brimmed headwear, such as a hat or bandana.

Steps:

- Don a hat with a brim.

- Put yourself where you can get the most sunshine.

- Let perspiration accumulate on the underside of the brim.

- Sweat will accumulate on your head if you don't tilt it to catch it.

**5. Tarps and other plastic sheets:**

Rainwater collection and the construction of solar stills both benefit from the use of plastic sheeting or tarps. How to modify them is as follows:

A. Catching Rainwater on Plastic Sheets:

Tarps, pebbles, and storage bins make up the material list.

Steps:

- The plastic sheeting or tarp should be spread out in the area where rainwater will be collected.

- You can secure the edges of the sheeting to the floor by using boulders or other heavy objects.

- You can collect water from the rain by placing containers in the indentations of the plastic sheeting.

B. Solar Still Covered with Plastic:

Supplies: a shovel, a plastic tarp, and a storage container.

Steps:

- Create a water well by excavating a hole.

- Make sure your container is centered in the opening.

- To hasten the process of evaporation, place wet plants or urine all around the container.

- Seal the hole with the plastic sheeting and weight it down with pebbles or dirt to keep out air.

- Sunlight causes water to evaporate from the ground, condense on the plastic, and eventually trickle into the storage container.

**6. Organic Components:**

It is possible to obtain water from natural sources when camping:

A. The Leaf Cone:

Large, hefty leaves (like banana leaves) serve as the material of choice.

Steps:

- Use a huge leaf and form it into a funnel.

- Use sticks or string to bind the edges together.

- Under a source of running water, such as dew or rain runoff, set up the leaf funnel.

**7. Pipes and tubes made of plastic:**

Well points can be dug using plastic tubes or pipes in sandy or loose soil.

A. Water Level:

We'll need some plastic tubing, a shovel, and a storage container.

Steps:

- Create a hole that goes below the water level.

- Put the pipe or tube into the opening.

- Cover the opening of the tube with a container.

- The tube will eventually become filled with groundwater from the surrounding area.

**8. Metal storage bins:**

Water collection and purification can be accomplished with metal containers:

A. Water Harvesting from Rain Using a Metal Container

Get a metal container, some duct tape, and some plastic tubing (if you like).

Steps:

- You can gather rainwater by positioning the metal container under a leaking tap or a running faucet.

- Make a spout by taping some plastic tubing over the opening of the container.

B. Bringing Water to a Boil in a Metal Pot:

Supplies: a metal container, some kind of flammable fuel, and some water.

Steps:

- Put water from wherever you can find it into the metal container.

- Boiling the water makes it safe to drink, so put it over a fire or other heat source.

# Chapter 2

# Filtration Fundamentals

## Diving into Filtration Systems

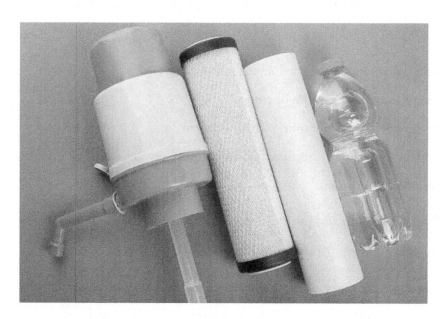

### Exploring Various Filtration Technologies and Their Applications

Filtration is an essential technique for purifying liquids and gases in a wide variety of applications. Filtration technologies serve critical roles in a wide range of fields, from the provision of clean drinking water and air to the improvement of manufacturing procedures. In this investigation, we will look into the many uses of filtration techniques.

**Filtration by Mechanical Means:**

Particles in a fluid can be physically removed via mechanical filtering by forcing the fluid through a barrier or media with predetermined pore sizes. The most widely used mechanical filtration methods include:

A. Filtration by Sand:

*Water Purification Systems*

- The principle of operation involves forcing water through a bed of sand or other granular materials, which collect and remove the suspended particles.
- Uses include filtration for swimming pools, purification of drinking water, and treatment of effluent.

B. Filtration in Depth:

*Filtration for Industrial Use*

- The principle of operation is based on the ability of porous materials like cellulose, diatomaceous earth, or activated carbon to retain particles at all levels.
- Application: Oil and gas purification, drug manufacturing, and the food and beverage industry.

C. Filtration via Membrane:

*Use For: Detoxifying And Cleaning*

- The principle at work here is the use of a thin, porous membrane with carefully controlled pore diameters to effect size-based particle separation.
- Ultrafiltration is used in the processing of milk and juice, microfiltration in the treatment of wastewater, and reverse osmosis for desalination.

**Biological Filtration System**

In biological filtration, microorganisms are used to degrade and remove pollutants from the air or water. Some of the most important technologies in this field are:

A. Filters That Slowly Drain:

*Purpose: Water Pollution Control*

- Methodology: Microbial biofilms feed on organic materials as wastewater trickles over a bed of rocks or plastic media.
- Common Applications: Septic Tanks and Municipal Wastewater Treatment Facilities.

B. Biofilters:

*Use For: Reducing Air Pollution*

- To remove gaseous contaminants, air is circulated across a bed of microorganisms (typically on organic material).
- Wastewater treatment odor control, industrial emission reduction.

**Filtration by Chemicals:**

In chemical filtration, chemicals are used to precipitate or react with contaminants, rendering them insoluble or facilitating their removal. Examples of common chemical filtration techniques include:

A. Flocculation and Coagulation:

*Water Purification Systems*

- The principle of operation is that the addition of chemicals (coagulants) to water will destabilize and aggregate tiny particles into larger flocs, which can then be more easily removed.

- Application: purifying drinking water and treating wastewater.

B. Filtration using Activated Carbon:

*Purification of Air and Water*

- Because of its high porosity and huge surface area, activated carbon is effective at removing contaminants from liquids and gases.

- Common applications include purifying drinking water, cleaning the air in your home, and cleaning the gas used in factories.

**EF:**

Particles in a fluid stream can be collected using electrostatic filtration, which makes use of electric charges to do so. There are primarily two approaches:

A. The Role of Electrostatic Precipitators

*Purpose: Regulating Air Quality*

- The particles are first electrically charged, and then they are collected on plates or surfaces that are electrically charged in the opposite direction.

- Uses include reducing dust and particles in the workplace and in coal-fired power plants.

B. Oil Filtration Using Electrostatic Forces:

*Use For: Oil Filtration and Industrial Lubrication*

- The principle of operation is based on the ability of an electric field to polarize and collect floating particles in oils and lubricants.

- Applications include filtration and oil purification in hydraulic systems.

**Separation using Ultrafiltration and Microfiltration:**

To filter out microscopic particles, colloids, and microbes, these methods use membranes with incredibly tiny pores.

A. Microfiltration:

*Biopharmaceuticals and the Food Industry*

- The principle of operation is that particles larger than 0.1 micrometers, such as bacteria, yeast, and viruses, are captured by the membrane's pores.

- Fruit juice clarification and drug manufacturing both benefit from the use of sterile filtering.

B. Ultrafiltration:

*Protein Isolation and Water Purification*

- The separation of dissolved solids, viruses, and proteins is achieved by using membranes with pores of 0.001 to 0.1 micrometers.

- Application: Deionization of water and biotech protein concentration

## Practical Tips for Building DIY Filtration Systems

DIY filtration system construction can be an inexpensive and informative approach to solving certain filtration problems. Here are some helpful hints to get you started on your quest to purify water for drinking, filter air, or separate solids from liquids:

### 1. Figure Out What Kind of Filtration You Need:

Find out which sediments, pollutants, bacteria, or chemicals must be eliminated from the fluid. Determine how much volume and how fast of a rate of flow your filtration system needs.

### 2. Round up your supplies:

Determine, in light of your filtration technique of choice, what supplies you will need for your do-it-yourself filtration endeavor. Always wear protective gear like gloves and goggles when handling chemicals or other potentially dangerous products.

### 3. Study Different Filtration Techniques

Consider your needs in light of the various filtering technologies (mechanical, biological, chemical, etc.) that have already been mentioned. Find the best filter media or membranes for your filtration process by doing some research.

### 4. Create a Filtration Plan:

Plan out your filtration system's layout and dimensions in great detail. Think about things like where filtration media or membranes will go and how they will link to the intake and outflow.

**5. Make sure it's set up securely:**

Construct a strong and safe enclosure for your filtration equipment. For more extensive endeavors, this is of paramount significance. Make sure there are no leaks by checking that all of your connections are airtight or watertight.

**6. Use Appropriate Filtering Media:**

To efficiently filter out your contaminants of interest, use a filtering medium or membrane with the right pore size and substance. If you want to increase the system's filtering efficiency and longevity, layering your media is a good idea.

**7. Pre-Filtering:**

Consider using a pre-filter to shield the primary filtration media or membrane from any large particles or trash in the source fluid. Pre-filters don't have to be complex devices.

**8. Scheduled Upkeep:**

Incorporate filter media cleaning and replacement into your regular maintenance routine. Keep an eye on the pressure differences across the filter, as an increase could mean that the filter is clogged.

**9. Recognize the Rate of Flow:**

Make sure the DIY filtration system you're planning on building can filter at the desired flow rate. Pumps may be needed to ensure sufficient flow rates for larger projects.

**10. Disinfect or clean the output ten**

To achieve potable water purity, it is recommended to add a final disinfection step, such as ultraviolet (UV) treatment or chemical disinfection (chlorination). The filtered product must be tested to ensure it is safe for the intended application.

**11. Take Safety Measures:**

Take all necessary precautions and wear protective gear when handling chemicals. Use caution around high-pressure systems and check that all parts can withstand the expected amount of force.

**12. Examine and Track:**

Make sure the quality of your homemade filtration system is up to par by testing the output on a regular basis. Document the filtration system's operation, upkeep, and changes.

**13. Get Professional Help:**

DIY filtration projects can be dangerous if you don't have the proper knowledge or equipment, so it's always best to check with specialists first.

**14. Begin with Easy Tasks:**

If you're just getting started with DIY filtering, it's best to tackle easier projects first so you may gain experience and confidence before moving on to more sophisticated systems.

**15. Record Your Construction:**

Document everything you can about how your filtration system was built and how well it has worked. You can use this record for future projects and troubleshooting.

**16. Taking the Environment into Account:**

Look into sustainable filtering media and materials that don't harm the environment.

If possible, think about how you may put the filtered materials to good use again.

**17. Learning and Teaching:**

To further understand filtration systems and methods, you should use educational materials including books, online guides, and courses.

**18. Conformity with Law and Regulations**

When dealing with potable water or industrial operations, it is extremely important to learn about and adhere to any municipal, state, or federal rules that may apply to your do-it-yourself filtration system.

**19. Ongoing Upgrading:**

Always be on the lookout for ways to improve the efficiency and efficacy of your do-it-yourself filtration system.

DIY filtration systems rely on careful planning, precise implementation, and consistent upkeep to function reliably over time. Achieving effective filtration solutions that are suited to your individual demands requires a methodical approach and careful attention to detail.

## Quick and Effective Filtration Methods in Crisis Situations

Having access to potable water is essential for survival in any kind of emergency. Water from a variety of sources can be made drinkable by using quick and effective filtration technologies. In the event of an emergency, consider the following filtration strategies:

**1. Simmering:**

When it comes to disinfecting water and killing hazardous germs, boiling is one of the most trusted procedures. It's useful for disinfecting water that would otherwise be harboring harmful microorganisms.

Steps:

- For at least one minute (or three minutes at higher elevations), ensure the water is at a rolling boil.
- Do not consume the water until it has cooled.

**2. Cloth filtration:**

Remove big particles and sediments from water by straining it through a clean cloth or fabric if you don't have access to specialized filters. It's an easy and fast way to get better water quality, but it won't work for everything.

Steps:

- Cover an object with a clean fabric or cloth.
- Strain the water through the cloth to remove any unwanted particles.
- Allow the filtered water to sit for a while so that any remaining sediment can sink to the bottom.
- Carefully transfer the purer water to a new container.

**3. Filtration by gravity:**

Simple materials and makeshift mechanisms can accomplish gravity filtration. Larger impurities can be removed and turbidity reduced, although it may not be as effective as commercial systems.

Steps:

- Look for two containers, one of which should have a tiny opening or spigot in the base.
- Wrap a clean cloth or several layers of cloth around the opening of the container.
- To fill the container with the hole, simply pour water through the cloth.
- The water can be filtered by gravity and collected in the spigot-equipped container.

**4. Make a filter out of sand and charcoal on the fly:**

It is possible to filter out sediments, organic materials, and even some chemicals with a simple sand and charcoal filter. Although it won't eliminate all disease-causing organisms, it can greatly enhance water quality.

Steps:

- Reduce a plastic bottle down to size to use as a filter container.
- Small rocks or pebbles go at the bottom of the container, then sand, and finally activated charcoal

(crushed charcoal from a fire).

- The contaminated liquid should be poured into the filter's top opening and allowed to trickle down through the media.
- Get the water that has been filtered at the bottom.

### 5. Removing Impurities Using Chemicals

When you can't boil the water for safety reasons, chemical purification is a good alternative. Tablets of iodine or chlorine bleach are frequently used alternatives.

#### Tablets of Iodine:

- To determine the correct dosage, read the label.
- Wait the suggested contact time (often 30 minutes) after dropping the tablet(s) into the water.
- To ensure even dispersion, stir or shake the container.
- It's okay to drink when the contact time has passed.

#### Cleaning with Chlorine:

- Regular household bleach containing 5.25 percent to 6 percent sodium hypochlorite should be used.
- Two drops of bleach for every quart (about 1 liter) of clear water, or four drops for hazy water.
- Toss and rest for at least half an hour.
- There should be a very slight chlorine smell in the water; if there isn't, add more and let it sit for 15 more minutes.

### SODIS (Solar Ocean Disinfection System):

SODIS is a straightforward technique that uses sunlight to disinfect water. Particularly helpful in sunny locales.

#### Steps:

- Put water into a clear plastic container but don't completely seal it.
- If it's a sunny day, leave the bottle out in the sun for 6 hours; if it's cloudy, leave it out for 2 days.
- The water will be purified by the sun's ultraviolet rays.

### 7. Portable commercial filters:

Water purifiers and filters made for outdoor or emergency usage are good at eliminating many different types of toxins from water, so utilize them if you have them. Many backpack-friendly filters are designed for use in both camping and emergency circumstances.

**8. Plato:**

Never, ever get the water you need to drink from locations like sewage treatment plants or stagnant ponds and puddles, especially if you can avoid doing so. Rather than that, you ought to center your efforts on obtaining your water supply from flowing streams and underground springs.

It is essential to keep in mind that different filtering methods, despite the fact that they can be beneficial in an emergency situation, do not necessarily guarantee that all pollutants will be removed. In situations where it is feasible to do so, filtration should be used in conjunction with other methods of water purification such as boiling and chemical disinfection. Additionally, you should be aware of the water condition in your region and pay attention to any instructions or cautions that your government may give regarding an emergency.

## Adapting Filtration Techniques to Different Water Qualities

To ensure that you can adequately cleanse and make water safe for consumption regardless of its source or original condition, it is essential to adapt filtration processes to those differences. Because of the wide range in water quality, it's important to have a firm grasp on how to fine-tune your filtration strategy. Here's how to modify filtration methods for use with water of varying quality:

### 1. Water that is devoid of sediment:

Mechanical Filtration, the Foundation of Filtration

Adaptation: Simple mechanical filtering methods can be used if the water is relatively clear and devoid of sediments or other obvious pollutants. Any leftover trash or particles can be easily filtered out with just a cloth or mesh screen.

### 2. Water that is cloudy or turbid:

Method of Filtration: Improved Mechanical Filtration

A multistage filtration system should be considered as an adaptation for water that is turbid, murky, or has visible particles in it. To begin, use a coarse filter to get rid of the bigger sediments, and then move on to a finer filter or cloth for the tinier stuff. When used repeatedly, this technique can greatly enhance water clarity.

### 3. The presence of bacteria:

Chemical and Biological Filtration as a Filtration Method

Adaptation: Use a combination of mechanical filtration and other purification procedures in the event that bacterial contamination of the water supply is suspected. Chemical disinfection (with chlorine or iodine, for example) is used to kill bacteria after mechanical filtering has removed solid particles. Boiling or UV sterilization as a secondary step can further ensure safety.

### 4. Chemical Pollutants:

A Filtration Method Using Activated Carbon

Activated carbon filtration is useful if you're worried about chemical pollutants, particularly those that alter taste and odor. Many different types of chemicals and organic molecules can be adsorbed using this technique. It is very helpful for enhancing the flavor of water that has been contaminated by industrial or agricultural waste.

### 5. Virus Infection:

Membrane filtration (pore sizes of 0.01 to 0.2 micrometers)

Viruses are much smaller than bacteria, thus they must be removed using membrane filtration with hole diameters between 0.01 and 0.2 micrometers. Safe drinking water can be protected from viruses in this way.

### 6. a lot of salt: brackish water:

Reverse osmosis and nanofiltration are two filtration methods.

Adaptation: Reverse osmosis or nanofiltration systems are required for highly salty water sources like brackish water or seawater. Desalinated water can be produced using these techniques.

### 7. Extremely murky and contaminated with bacteria:

The Use of Multiple Filtration Stages

Adaptation: When dealing with water that is both cloudy and perhaps infected with germs, a multistage filtering method is necessary. Remove big sediments first with a coarse filter, then smaller particles with a finer filter. Then, move on to eliminating germs and viruses with chemical disinfection. Finally, activated carbon or ultraviolet (UV) treatment can be used to further improve water quality.

### 8. Severe Pollution:

Methods of Filtration That Work Together

Adaptation: Multiple filtering processes may be required to address severe water quality problems such the presence of heavy metals, industrial pollutants, or radioactive elements. Consult a professional and think about installing a filter system designed to get rid of the particular toxins there.

### 9. Water from Unreliable Sources:

Adaptation: In times of crisis or survival, it's important to have a plan for dealing with water of varying quality. Have on hand a filtering system that can adapt to different environments and different kinds of pollutants. In these cases, a portable, all-in-one filter with numerous filtration stages and chemical treatment options would be extremely helpful.

**10. Always Keeping an Eye Out:**

It is essential to routinely verify the quality of the water that has been filtered, despite the fact that the water's origin or starting point does not matter. You can use a test kit or another type of device to assess whether or not the water in your home is suitable for human consumption.

To protect drinking water supplies, recreational water areas, and aquatic ecosystems, it is essential to have in place rigorous water quality monitoring and treatment procedures. When adapting filtration techniques to varied water qualities, it is vital to select the appropriate filter type and purification processes to address specific contaminants and issues. When faced with an emergency situation in which the water quality may be compromised, it is of the utmost importance to put safety first and make use of a tiered strategy to ensure that the filtered water satisfies all of your health and safety requirements.

# Chapter 3

# Purification Mastery

## Chemical Purification Demystified

### Comprehensive Guide to Chemical Purification Methods

Chemical purification techniques are essential for making water fit for human consumption and for use in a wide range of industrial applications. Chemical treatments are used in this context to purify liquids by destroying harmful microorganisms and other pollutants. In this detailed tutorial, we'll learn about the many chemical purification techniques, how they work, and where you may put them to use.

### 1. Chlorination:

Chlorination, in which chlorine compounds like chlorine gas ($Cl2$) or sodium hypochlorite ($NaClO$) are added to water, is a common chemical purification process. Chlorine is widely used as a disinfectant due to its ability to destroy or inactivate bacteria, viruses, and numerous parasites.

Mechanism:

- Hypochlorous acid (HOCl) and hypochlorite ions (OCl-) are produced when chlorine combines with water.

- These chemicals are powerful oxidants that destroy bacteria by damaging their cell membranes and metabolic processes.

Applications:

- Treatment of water supplied by the municipality.

- Cleaning and sanitizing aquatic facilities.

- Cleaning water for commercial use.

- Water purification in an emergency.

## 2. Ozone depletion:

Water can be disinfected with both organic and inorganic contaminants removed by a chemical process called ozonation, which makes use of ozone (O3), a potent oxidizing agent. Ozone purification is excellent at destroying a wide variety of pollutants.

Mechanism:

- Separated ozone molecules react with organic molecules, leading to their breakdown.

- Furthermore, it oxidizes and kills bacteria by causing cellular disruption.

Applications:

- Safe and clean drinking water.

- Treatment of sewage.

- Processing of food and drink.

- Healthcare drug manufacturing.

## 3. UV Sterilization:

Ultraviolet (UV) disinfection is a chemical-free alternative that employs UV light to kill germs and viruses in water. The water is not treated with any chemicals.

Mechanism:

- Microorganisms' DNA and RNA are damaged by ultraviolet radiation, rendering them incapable of replicating and spreading disease.

- UV disinfection just kills bacteria; it does not affect any other contaminants in the water.

Applications:

- Public water purification systems.

- Water purifying systems for individual usage.

- Locations of medical care.

- Fish aquaculture and other aquatic cultivation.

## 4. Coagulation and Flocculation:

Water treatment facilities use the chemical process of coagulation-flocculation to filter out suspended particles, colloids, and even certain dissolved chemicals. In order to make the water's particles larger and therefore easier to filter out, coagulants and flocculants are added to the water.

Mechanism·

- Particles can be rendered less stable by coagulants such aluminum sulfate and ferric chloride by canceling out their surface charges.

- The use of flocculants (such as polymers) facilitates the coalescence of particles into larger, more easily settled flocs.

Applications:

- Safe and clean drinking water.

- Treatment of sewage.

- Manufacturing techniques (like those used in mining and paper making).

- Reclaiming water from the surface for human consumption.

## 5. Exchanging Ions:

Water hardness ions like calcium and magnesium can be chemically removed via an ion exchange system. The process entails pumping water across a resin bed containing ion-exchange media.

Mechanism:

- Water ions with the opposite charge are attracted to the charged sites in ion exchange resins and are bound to them.

- The resin bed acts as a filter, exchanging the ions in the water for those released by the resin.

Applications:

- Treatment to lessen the hardness of water.

- Water demineralization for manufacturing uses.

- Decontamination from radioactive and heavy metals.

- Manufacturing ultra-pure water for use in sensitive electronics and medications.

### 6. Absorbance:

By attracting and attaching them to its surface, an adsorbent can pull compounds that are dissolved or suspended in a liquid (adsorbate) out of the liquid. Water purification systems often use activated carbon as a typical adsorbent.

Mechanism:

- Activated carbon is an adsorbent material with a high surface area and a high number of binding sites.

- Adsorbed onto the carbon's surface are organic pollutants, some compounds, and even scents.

Applications:

- Substances that alter water's flavor and smell are eliminated.

- Lessening the concentration of organic pollutants in factory runoff.

- The sanitization of indoor air.

- VOC (volatile organic compound) removal from contaminated groundwater.

### 7. Rain:

It is possible to separate precipitate particles by sedimentation or filtering after they have been precipitated by adding chemicals that react with certain ions in water to generate insoluble solid particles.

Mechanism:

- Lime or alum, two examples of precipitants, are added to the water.

- Solid precipitates are formed when precipitants react with ions such as phosphate, sulfate, or heavy metals.

- These particles are heavy enough to either filter out of the water or sink to the bottom.

Applications:

- Metal recovery from municipal wastewater.

- Removing phosphates from municipal wastewater.

- Mine drainage sulfate levels are being lowered.

### 8. Neutralization:

Neutralization is used to put water's pH into a specified range by adding acids or bases. The effectiveness of following treatment operations can be greatly enhanced as well as corrosion in distribution systems can be avoided if this is done.

Mechanism:

- To adjust the pH of water, either an acid or a base is used.

- Substances with an acidic or alkaline pH are neutralized by a series of chemical reactions.

Applications:

- Correction of drinking water pH during purification.

- Remediation of Acid Mine Drainage.

- pH regulation in manufacturing settings.

## 9. Reducing Disinfectant By Products (DBP):

Managing the development of disinfection byproducts (DBPs) such trihalomethanes (THMs) and haloacetic acids (HAAs) that might occur during chlorination or ozonation is important, but it is not water purification in and of itself.

Mechanism:

- Reduce how often you use chlorine or ozone.

- Disinfect with UV or chlorine dioxide if those other options aren't available.

- Disinfecting a surface requires the removal of precursors (organic matter).

Applications:

- The treatment of drinking water should minimize the production of DBPs.

- Maintaining potable water standards in accordance with government mandates.

## 10. AOPs (Advanced Oxidation Processes):

Water pollutants can be eliminated with the use of powerful oxidants like hydrogen peroxide ($H_2O_2$) and ozone by the use of advanced oxidation technologies. When it comes to dismantling tough organic molecules, AOPs really shine.

Mechanism:

- Powerful oxidizing species are produced by the reaction of strong oxidants with UV light or other catalysts, and these species react with and breakdown pollutants.

Applications:

- Refractory organic compound treatment for industrial wastewater.

- Purification of wastewater by removing medicines and personal care goods.

- Remediation of polluted aquifers.

## Best Practices and Safety Measures in Chemical Purification

Water and other liquids' purity and safety are dependent on chemical purification techniques. However, there are risks associated with dealing with chemicals that must be mitigated to safeguard human and environmental health. Safe and efficient chemical purification is the goal of this book, and to that end, we'll examine best practices and safety procedures.

### 1. Safe Chemical Storage and Handling:

Make sure that everyone who works with chemicals in the purification process has received thorough training in the proper handling of chemicals, safety measures, and emergency drills.

Compatibility between Chemicals:

- Keep Chemicals Together That Can Be! Collect and maintain a complete set of safety data sheets (SDS) and chemical inventory records.

- Chemicals should be kept in cool, dark places away from sources of heat and light, as well as incompatible materials.

Labeling:

- Clearly indicate the contents, hazard warnings, and storage requirements on all chemical containers.

- To prevent chemical spills from entering the environment, secondary containment devices (such as spill containment pallets) can be used.

### 2. safety gear for yourself:

Pick the right personal protective equipment (PPE) for the chemicals you'll be working with, such as gloves, safety goggles or face shields, lab coats, and chemical-resistant aprons. Make that personal protective equipment (PPE) fits, is comfortable, and is periodically inspected for damage. Provide readily available emergency equipment like eyewash stations and safety showers, and make sure you test and maintain them periodically.

### 3. Mechanical Airflow and Architectural Regulations:

To get rid of chemical odors and airborne particles in enclosed spaces, set up local exhaust ventilation systems. Use a fume hood, which is a ventilated, enclosed enclosure, when working with flammable or toxic substances. In the event of a chemical spill or other emergency, it is crucial that all machinery and procedures have failsafes in place to immediately shut down production.

## 4. Management of Chemical Stocks:

Conduct periodic audits of chemical inventories to identify substances that have expired, become obsolete, or have degraded beyond use. Keep chemicals in separate containers to avoid any accidental mixing or reactions. Reduce the amount of chemicals stored to lessen the impact of any leaks or mishaps.

## 5. Risk Analysis and Mitigation:

Conduct a comprehensive hazard analysis of all chemicals employed in the purification process to determine which ones pose the greatest danger. Risk reduction is achieved by taking preventative steps, such as installing containment systems, barriers, and automatic shut-off devices. Prepare and disseminate a comprehensive emergency action plan that details how to handle a spill, how to safely evacuate the area, and how to get in touch with the proper authorities.

## 6. Methods for Safely Handling Chemicals:

Clearly identify containers and record all steps taken to handle chemicals, including amounts used and how long they took to react. To prevent unwanted chemical reactions, substances should be added in the correct order. Incorporate chemicals cautiously and gradually. To avoid any unwanted reactions or contamination, always use clean equipment and containers while working with chemicals.

## 7. Prevention and Control of Oil and Chemical Releases:

Measures for Containing SpillsPlace absorbent materials and spill berms in places where chemical spills are possible. Urgent Action: Respond swiftly to chemical spills in accordance with standard spill response protocols. Keep people out, spread the word, and start cleaning up. Protecting Employees' Health and Safety Make sure all spill response workers have access to necessary safety gear and protective clothing.

## 8. Disposal of Garbage:

Sort trash into bins marked "hazardous" and "non-hazardous," respectively. Disposal must follow municipal, state, and federal guidelines for the proper disposal of hazardous materials.

## 9. Instruction and Study:

Conduct ongoing training for all employees involved in chemical purification processes, covering topics such as chemical safety, emergency procedures, and best practices. Make sure that everyone who comes into contact with the chemicals in the workplace is aware of the risks involved and knows how to protect themselves.

**10. Upkeep and Checkups:**

Inspect and maintain all pumps, valves, pipes, and filtration systems utilized in chemical purification on a regular basis. Maintain thorough inspection and maintenance records for all equipment to assure dependability and head off problems before they arise.

## Leveraging UV and Solar Power for Water Purification

Sustainable and environmentally friendly methods for making water safe to drink include those that utilize natural filtration processes like UV (ultraviolet) light and solar electricity. These methods use sunshine and ultraviolet (UV) radiation to purify water by killing dangerous bacteria, viruses, and other organisms. This book will delve further into the mechanisms and applications of UV and solar power as they pertain to water purification.

### 1. Purifying Water with Ultraviolet Radiation (UV):

UV water purification is a tried-and-true method of chemical-free water disinfection. UV-C light is used for its germicidal characteristics to eliminate or deactivate waterborne pathogens.

Mechanism:

- The DNA and RNA of microbes are damaged by UV-C radiation (with wavelengths between 200 and 280 nanometers), rendering them unable to reproduce and spread disease.

- UV-C light disrupts the cellular structure of microorganisms, rendering them harmless, by absorption by their genetic material.

Applications:

- UV systems are commonly used as a secondary disinfection method at municipal water treatment facilities.

- Home water purification systems using ultraviolet radiation can guarantee the quality of the water your family drinks.

- UV systems are used to disinfect process water in numerous industrial settings, such as the food and beverage, pharmaceutical, and electronics manufacturing industries.

- Effluent water from sewage treatment plants can be treated with ultraviolet light to kill any remaining bacteria or viruses before being released back into the environment.

- Water used for patient care and equipment sterilization in hospitals and other healthcare institutions is purified using UV disinfection.

The Benefits of Using UV Light to Clean Water:

- There are no chemical residues or flavor changes because no chemicals were used.

- It kills a large variety of bacteria and viruses, including some that are resistant to chlorine.

- Applications large and small will benefit from its low energy consumption and low cost.

- Lamp replacement is the only regular maintenance that is needed.

- Sustainable and low impact on the planet.

**Relying on the Sun to Purify Water (SODIS):**

In sunny regions, clean drinking water can be easily obtained by the use of solar disinfection, commonly known as Solar Water Disinfection (SODIS). It uses the sun's heat and UV-A rays to disinfect water and make it safe to drink.

Mechanism:

- Sunlight's ultraviolet (UV-A) rays can pass through water and react with organic molecules, releasing oxygen radicals (ROS) such hydrogen peroxide and hydroxyl radicals.

- Free radicals (ROS) damage the cell membranes and DNA of bacteria, killing them.

- By increasing the temperature of the water, solar heating helps in the disinfection process by killing off any remaining pathogens.

- Procedures for Solar Ozone Disinfection of Water (SODIS):

- Pick PET (polyethylene terephthalate) bottles that are see-through, and then pour the sterilized water into them. Since PET bottles effectively transmit UV-A radiation, they come highly recommended.

- The bottles should be exposed to sunlight for at least 6 hours on a sunny day, or 2 days on an overcast day. To get the most UV exposure, the bottles should be laid flat.

- Solar heating raises water's temperature, which helps kill off disease-causing microorganisms. Temperatures could rise to over 122 degrees Fahrenheit (50 degrees Celsius) in the sun.

- Seal the bottle tops to keep out contaminants before, during, and after disinfection.

- For best results, wait at least 30 minutes after solar exposure before drinking the cleaned water. This buys some time for any lingering ROS to finish up the disinfection.

SODIS (Solar Ozone Depletion Disinfection of Water) Uses:

- Household Water Treatment: In areas where there is a scarcity of clean water sources, SODIS is commonly employed.

- It's a great way to clean water in a pinch, especially in disaster-stricken countries where supplies are few.

- Non-governmental organizations (NGOs) and humanitarian organizations (ONGOs) frequently promote and conduct SODIS initiatives in areas where residents lack access to clean water.

- Activities in the great outdoors: Backpackers and other travelers can use SODIS to purify water from streams and other untreated water sources.

SODIS (Solar Optimized Disinfection of Water Systems) Benefits:

- Easy to come by and cheap, all you need is some clear PET bottles and some sunlight.

- Easy to implement, even in places where resources are scarce.

- safe for the planet because it doesn't require any harmful chemicals or expensive machinery.

- A wide variety of aquatic pathogens are rendered inert.

- Encourages people to get involved in cleaning up their water supply.

**Factors to Think About When Purifying Water with UV and Solar Energy:**

The effectiveness of ultraviolet (UV) and solar (S) water filtration systems is enhanced by the presence of clear, transparent water. Pre-filtering turbid or muddy water can make these techniques more effective.

- Higher water temperatures facilitate more efficient solar disinfection. It may be required to switch to a different approach or install extra heating in areas with colder winters.

- Choose suitable containers for both approaches. Non-transparent materials will block UV-C light, hence UV systems must use transparent tubes made of quartz or glass. PET bottles are ideal for sun disinfection because to their high UV-A transmission rates.

- When compared to UV systems, which give rapid disinfection in seconds to minutes, solar disinfection can take many hours to provide appropriate disinfection.

- Ensure the efficacy of the purifying process by putting in place stringent systems of monitoring and quality control. In order to detect lamp failures or insufficient UV dosages, UV systems should be outfitted with UV intensity sensors and alarms.

- UV systems require regular upkeep, such as the periodic replacement of lamps and the cleaning of quartz sleeve or tube fixtures. Keep the SODIS bottles clean and free of biofilm at all times.

- UV-C rays can cause skin and eye damage and should be avoided. When working with UV systems, it's important to take precautions and wear protective gear.

# Integrating Nature's Purification Processes into Your Strategy

There are many natural purification mechanisms available to humans, each of which has evolved over millions of years to keep ecosystems healthy and pristine. Harnessing and incorporating these natural processes into diverse techniques can help solve environmental problems, increase sustainability, and boost people's quality of life. Whether your goal is clean water, responsible waste disposal, or environmentally sound farming, we'll cover the best ways to incorporate nature's purifying processes into your plan.

## 1. Water Filtration Methods Derived From Nature

### A. Wetlands

Constructed wetlands should be incorporated into municipal and industrial wastewater treatment systems as an integration strategy. Wetlands have many positive effects, including the filtration and purification of water, the removal of nutrients and toxins, and the capture of sediments. They provide as a home for several animal species as well.

### B. Zones of Riparian Protection:

Agricultural and urban runoff can be filtered by establishing riparian buffer zones along water bodies as part of an integration strategy. By capturing sediments, nutrients, and pollutants before they may enter water bodies, buffer zones are beneficial in reducing pollution. They improve the quality of water sources and encourage biodiversity.

### C. Plant-Based Remediation:

Use phytoremediation to purify polluted water and soil as part of your integration strategy. Advantages Pollutants, such as heavy metals and organic compounds, can be absorbed, accumulated, and broken down by plants like sunflowers, willows, and poplars, making this method of remediation successful and sustainable.

## 2. Agricultural Sustainability:

### A. Rotating Crops:

Crop rotation strategies, which replicate natural ecosystems and increase soil health, are an integral part of this integration strategy. Crop rotation's advantages include a lower need for synthetic fertilizers and pesticides, improved nutrient cycling, and the prevention of pests and diseases.

### B. Agroforestry:

Crop productivity can be diversified, shade can be provided, and soil fertility can be increased by including trees and shrubs into agricultural settings. The advantages of agroforestry systems include increased biodiversity, carbon sequestration, and increased resistance to the effects of climate change.

C. Protective Crops:

Strategy for incorporating: use cover crops during fallow times to preserve and enhance soil quality. Benefits include healthier soils and less nutrient runoff due to less erosion, fewer weeds, and fixed nitrogen from cover crops.

### 3. Controlling Garbage:

A. Composting:

Organic waste composting is a natural approach to recycle nutrients and cut down on landfill waste, hence it should be encouraged as part of the integration strategy. Composting's many advantages include lowering GHG emissions and bolstering sustainable agriculture by transforming organic waste into nutrient-rich soil additives.

B. Methods of Anaerobic Digestion:

Organic waste can be recycled into energy in the form of biogas and nutrient-rich digestate through the integration of anaerobic digestion systems. Among its many advantages, anaerobic digestion helps cut down on harmful methane gas released by landfills, creates sustainable energy, and makes useful fertilizers for farmers.

C. Biological cleanup:

Use microbial and fungal bioremediation strategies to clean up polluted groundwater and soil. Using bioremediation to clean up polluted areas is beneficial since it is more cost-effective and long-lasting than other methods.

### 4. Biomass Power:

Use biomass such as wood, farm waste, and algae to produce sustainable energy as part of your integration strategy. Greenhouse gas emissions can be reduced because biomass energy doesn't produce any, and it can be used instead of, fossil fuels in power generation.

Energy from the Sun:

Use photovoltaic panels and solar thermal systems to collect and store energy from the sun as part of your integration strategy. Solar energy has many advantages, including lowering energy costs and decreasing reliance on finite fossil resources.

Utilizing Wind Power:

Wind turbines should be installed as part of the integration strategy in order to harness wind energy and convert it into electricity.

*Advantages:*

Wind power helps achieve energy independence and lowers pollution levels without producing any harmful pollutants.

## 5. EbA (or adaptation based on ecosystems):

In terms of a. afforestation and reforestation,

Strategy for Combination: Fund reforestation and afforestation initiatives to bring back forest cover and reduce the effects of global warming. Forests play an important role in climate resilience because of the carbon they store, the water they control, and the other ecosystem services they give.

Restoring a Coastal Area:

Strategy for integrating protection against coastal erosion and storm surges through the restoration of coastal ecosystems like mangroves, salt marshes, and coral reefs.

Advantages:

Coastal ecosystems mitigate the effects of storms, safeguard coastlines, and sustain fish populations.

Environmentally Responsible Land Use:

Adopt sustainable land management approaches to protect soil health, lessen erosion, and maintain biodiversity as an integration strategy.

Food security, water quality, and climate change resilience are all strengthened by sustainable land management practices.

## 6. Sustainable City Design:

A. Green Infrastructure:

Green roofs, urban parks, and permeable pavements can all be integrated into city planning as a means of controlling runoff and mitigating the effects of heat islands. Green infrastructure is advantageous because it strengthens cities, reduces the likelihood of flooding, and raises the standard of living in urban areas.

B. Farming in the City:

Strategy for integrating: support urban agriculture for better local food production, shorter food supply chains, and more resilient cities. The advantages of urban agriculture include the availability of healthy, locally grown food, the prevention of wasted food, and increased participation in civic life.

C. Protecting Biodiversity:

Protect and restore urban biodiversity through the development of wildlife corridors, urban green spaces, and wildlife-friendly landscaping; this is the integration strategy. Advantages include increased ecological resilience, increased pollination, and improvements to urban aesthetics and quality of life.

**7. Efficient Water Use:**

A. Harvesting Rainwater:

Rainwater harvesting systems that collect and store rainwater for later use is one integration strategy. Rainwater collection has many advantages, including water conservation, reduced storm water runoff, and a reliable water supply.

B. Filtration by Nature:

Strategy for Incorporation: Advocate for the use of vegetated swales and built wetlands as natural filtration solutions for handling stormwater runoff. Natural filtration helps clean up water, make it safer for aquatic life, and increase the value of aquatic ecosystems.

C. Recharging of Aquifers:

Integrate strategies for recharging subsurface aquifers (known as managed aquifer recharge, or MAR). The availability of water is increased, groundwater levels are maintained, and the effects of groundwater depletion are reduced thanks to MAR systems.

**7. Awareness and Learning:**

Promoting education and awareness campaigns to educate communities, businesses, and legislators on the value of incorporating natural purifying processes into a wide range of methods is a key component of the integration strategy. Advantages Raise in environmental consciousness can lead to more widespread adoption of environmentally friendly behaviors and policies.

**8. Difficulties and Things to Think About:**

There are many advantages to incorporating nature's purifying processes into different tactics, but there are also some obstacles and things to think about. Consider the potential trade-offs between economic growth and environmental protection. Long-term viability requires a compromise that accommodates both of these competing goals.

Policy and Regulation:

Develop policies and regulations, and make sure they are firmly enforced, that encourage the use of natural purification processes and other ecologically friendly methods of operation. Participation of local communities and important stakeholders in decision-making processes helps ensure that resulting plans are inclusive of all relevant parties and show respect for cultural norms. It is possible to evaluate the effectiveness of integrated solutions with the assistance of monitoring and evaluation systems, both of which must to be put into place. Invest in research and development to come up with innovative answers to long-standing issues and improved strategies for integrating naturally occurring cleansing procedures into previously developed blueprints.

# Chapter 4

# Efficient Storage Solutions

## Selecting Appropriate Containers

https://img.freepik.com/free-photo/manual-worker-warehouse_329181-12789.jpg?size=626&ext=jpg&ga=GA1.1.844631866.1696529323&semt=ais

### Assessing Container Options for Long-Term Water Storage

Choosing the right containers for long-term water storage is essential for maintaining the water's integrity and freshness. If you're stocking up on water for emergencies, off-the-grid living, or outdoor activities, the containers you use will have a major impact on how that water holds up over time. When deciding between several containers, it is important to think about the following:

**1. Material:**

A. High-Density Polyethylene (HDPE) Plastics, Used in the Food Industry:

HDPE containers are advantageous due to its low weight, sturdiness, and resistance to chemicals and ultraviolet light. They don't change the way the water tastes or smells in any way.

Con: Plastic containers can fade in direct sunshine and fracture under freezing weather. For long-term storage in the sun, select plastics that won't fade.

B. It's Made of Glass:

The water will not be contaminated because glass is impermeable. It can withstand exposure to sunlight and won't deteriorate with time. Glass bottles and jars have a number of drawbacks that make them unsuitable for use in the great outdoors or in an emergency.

C. Steel, Stainless:

Stainless steel water containers last a long time, don't rust, and don't change the taste or smell of

THE NEW PREPPER'S WATER SURVIVAL BIBLE

the water in any way. They may be kept for a long time and used outside without deteriorating. The drawbacks of stainless-steel storage containers are their weight and price.

## 2. Ability to Hold:

Pick for storage units that have the right amount of space for your requirements. Think on how much water you'll need for daily needs like drinking, cooking, and washing. Larger containers may be better for long-term storage, but they might be difficult to move about once they're full.

## 3. Sealing Capacity:

Make sure the container is tightly sealed to avoid spillage and spoilage. Common features to check for include caps that screw on, gaskets, or sealed lids.

## 4. Resilience:

Pick for storage bins that can withstand the test of time and are built to last. Try to find goods that have a history of satisfying customers and lasting for a long time.

## 5. openness:

If you can, use containers with a see-through quality. Without even opening the bottle, you can see if the water is clear or if there are any symptoms of contamination.

## 6. Portability:

Think about how easily the containers can be moved around. Choose water storage containers with handles or wheels for portability when on the move.

## 7. UV Shielding:

Choose containers with UV protection or store the containers in a shady place to avoid UV damage when storing water outside or in locations exposed to sunshine.

## 8. Capacity to Stack:

Choose stackable containers if you need to save on storage space. When closet space is at a premium, this function might be invaluable.

## 9. It's Simple to Clean:

Wide-mouthed containers are less of a pain to disinfect after use. Make sure there is an easy way to clean the container so that germs doesn't grow in it.

## 10. Food-safe and BPA-free:

Make sure the plastic containers you use are both BPA-free and marked as safe for use with food. This prevents toxins from the plastic from seeping into the water supply.

## 11. Keeping warm:

Water held in insulated containers can be protected from freezing or overheating in situations with extreme temperatures.

## 12. Airflow:

It is possible to avoid spillage and contamination during dispensing by using a spigot or other type of vent found on some containers.

## 13. Legality in the U.S.

Make sure the FDA or your country's equivalent has given their stamp of approval on any containers or materials that will be in touch with water.

## 14. Routine Checkups:

Checking stored water for symptoms of contamination including discolouration, off-odors, or strange tastes is important regardless of the container used to keep it. Keep the water fresh by switching it out every so often.

## 15. Water Purification System:

Water should be treated to eliminate any microorganisms before being stored. Water purification tablets, boiling, and filtering are all viable options, albeit their efficacy depends on the quality of the source water.

## 16. Maintenance and Cleaning Procedures:

Maintain your storage units by cleaning them frequently. Before using again, wash them in detergent-free water, rinse them well, and let them dry completely. Be sure to clean and sanitize any lids or tops as well.

## 17. Where:

Keep containers out of the reach of children and pets, and away from excessive temperatures and any possible sources of contamination by storing them in a cold, dark, and dry place. Containers can be protected from pests and dampness by keeping them off the ground.

## 18. Circulation:

Water that will be held for an extended amount of time should be recirculated every so often. This procedure helps guarantee the water remains fresh and safe to consume.

# Space-Saving Techniques

## Innovative Storage Solutions for Limited Spaces

When prepping for crises or off-grid life in small spaces, it's extremely important to maximize storage efficiency. Here are some space-saving strategies for handling water issues:

**1. Water bottles that can be stacked:**

Invest in water containers that can be stacked on top of each other to save valuable floor space. These containers' construction and durability must be geared toward the long-term storage of water.

**2. Attached to the wall shelves:**

If you're short on floor space but still need to store a lot of water bottles, place some shelves on the wall. Smaller containers, water purification equipment, and other survival necessities can be stored on wall shelves.

**3. Storing Things Under the Bed:**

Put water containers or a water purification kit under your bed in case of an emergency. There are watertight containers and drawers made to fit neatly beneath most mattresses.

**4. Concealed Cupboards:**

You could quietly store water supplies in your home by building hidden or disguised cupboards. These cabinets are both stylish and functional, as they can be painted to match any room's color scheme.

**5. Space-Saving Filtration Devices:**

Try to get a water filtration system that is small enough to fit into the available area. Safe drinking water is easily accessible with the help of these systems, and they don't take up much room.

**6. Modules for Organizing Stuff:**

Consider using storage modules that can be adjusted to fit the available area. Adjustable shelves are a common feature of these multipurpose units, allowing them to accommodate a variety of container sizes.

**7. Door-mounted racks:**

Hang over-the-door shoe racks or organizers with pockets over the door to store emergency water bags, water testing kits, and purification tablets.

**8. Folding water bottles:**

Foldable or collapsible water containers are a great option for short-term or on-the-go storage. These may be folded down when not in use and enlarged when necessary.

**9. Compact dispensing devices:**

Make use of wall- or counter-mounted water dispensers to avoid taking up precious floor area while yet providing easy access to water.

**10. Roll-Out Racks:**

You can make it easier to get to things in the rear of your cabinets if they are stored there by installing roll-out racks or shelves.

## Maximizing Storage Efficiency for Emergency Preparedness

Planning and organization are crucial for successful emergency preparedness, especially when it comes to storing life-sustaining necessities like food, water, and shelter. Maximizing storage efficiency is crucial for ensuring that necessary supplies can be accessed in the event of an emergency. Make the most of your emergency supplies storage space with these tips!

**1. Focus on What's Most Important:**

To get started, it's important to determine which emergency supplies are vital. Typical items include h2o, nonperishable food, first aid supplies, lighting, batteries, gadgets, and paperwork. Putting the essentials first helps you make the most effective use of your time and resources.

**2. Methods of Water Conservation:**

One of the most essential resources for human survival is water. In order to make the most of water storage space:

- Purchase water containers that stack and are BPA-free so you can save room in a small area.
- Put your water bottles under your bed.
- You could want to put some shelves on the wall to keep water on.
- Use barrels or water storage tanks that are made for long-term use.
- Keep water supplies fresh by switching them out on a regular basis.

### 3. Portable refrigerators:

When putting away dry goods:

- To save space, choose foods that are vacuum-sealed or packaged singly.
- To keep insects out of your dry products, store them in see-through, airtight containers.
- To keep food fresh for a longer period of time, use oxygen absorbers and Mylar bags.
- Select items that are both compact and nutritious, such as dried fruit, cereals, and canned goods.

### 4. Storage & Racking That's Easily Modified:

Get yourself some modular shelving units with movable shelves so you may organize your stock the way you want. These storage spaces are adaptable and may house a wide range of container dimensions.

### 5. Vertical Racks:

Make the most of your walls by installing shelves, hooks, and racks to store your belongings. Put supplies and products that don't weigh much higher up on the shelf.

### 6. Unused Areas:

Find the unused parts of your house or garage and put them to good use:

- Water containers, sleeping bags, and emergency supplies can all find a home under a bed.
- Shelving and hooks are two common accessories for closets.
- Small goods like first aid kits and flashlights can be stored in over-the-door holders.

### 7. Roll-Out Racking:

The back shelves of cupboards and closets can be reached with the help of roll-out storage solutions. Canned goods and other kitchen supplies may benefit greatly from these.

### 8. Packages that are hermetically sealed with a vacuum:

Clothing, bedding, and other soft goods can be compressed by placing them in vacuum-sealed bags. This not only keeps plants safe from moisture and pests, but also decreases the amount of space they require.

### 9. Labeling and stocktaking:

Labeling all containers and keeping an accurate inventory will help you keep your system running smoothly. In a time of crisis, being able to rapidly locate specific products is crucial.

**10. Check and rotate your supplies frequently:**

Inspect storage equipment and food for signs of damage or spoilage on a regular basis. Make sure your emergency stockpile is always reliable by rotating perishable goods and replacing expired products as necessary.

**11. Furniture with Multiple Uses:**

Think about getting pieces of furniture that can serve multiple purposes. Storage ottomans and beds with drawers or lift-up mattresses are only two examples.

**12. Effective Packing Techniques:**

Use compression sacks or packing cubes to save space and keep your emergency supplies neatly arranged while you're on the go.

**13. Save Room with These Appliances:**

Choose portable gadgets that can nevertheless get the job done, such as a hand-cranked radio or a small stove.

**14. Robust Storage:**

Purchase high-quality, long-lasting storage containers. To keep your materials safe, use containers that can withstand moisture and insects.

**15. Turn it over and start over:**

Evaluate your stock of emergency supplies on a regular basis to make sure nothing has expired and that everything is in good operating shape. Keep your readiness levels at an optimal level by replacing or restocking as needed.

The effectiveness of your emergency supplies storage can be improved by using the aforementioned methods. You can feel more at ease knowing that you and your loved ones are protected in the event of an emergency thanks to your well-organized storage space.

# Chapter 5

# Integration and Tactical Approaches

## Crafting Your Holistic Off-Grid Hydration Plan

### Developing a Personalized Water Survival Strategy

The availability of clean water is crucial in situations requiring off-grid survival or disaster preparedness. Depending on your unique set of conditions, you'll require a different approach to water survival. Here's a step-by-step manual for developing your own personal, off-the-grid water supply strategy:

**1. Take Stock of Your Predicament:**

Determine first what your specific needs are:

- My question is, where do you call home? Think about the weather and where you can get water.

- How many individuals make up your family or group? Find out how much water each person requires each day.

- How long will you be without power due to an outage or other emergency? Prepare for both the immediate and distant future.

- Is there anything about your health or diet that prevents you from drinking a lot of water?

**2. Figure Out How Much Water You'll Need:**

Depending on the size of your group and the weather forecast, calculate how much water you'll need each day. One gallon (3.8 liters) per person, per day is the recommended minimum amount of water for daily use in drinking and sanitation. Make necessary adjustments here.

### 3. Water Collection and Its Origins:

Determine where water might be obtained:

- Think about installing gutters and water tanks to collect rainwater for later use.

- If you live near a body of water like a lake, river, or stream, you should create a system to filter the water.

- If you have access to a well, make sure it is in good operating shape and think about getting a manual pump.

- Put water in containers that can keep it fresh for a long time.

### 4. Purifying and filtering water:

Make your collected water fit for human consumption by investing in filter and purification systems:

- To filter water, just use a portable filter that can handle the job.

- When you boil water, you destroy hazardous germs.

- Tablets or liquid solutions such as chlorine dioxide are chemical options for treating water.

- Ultraviolet (UV) purifiers have been shown to be effective against germs and viruses.

- Purify water by passing it through a distillation apparatus.

### 5. Space-Saving Methods:

Choose the right containers for storing water:

- Lightweight and convenient for short- to medium-term storage, BPA-free plastic containers are an excellent option.

- Larger containers are preferable for long-term water storage, such as food-grade barrels or drums.

- Think about labeling and rotation to keep things recognizable and fresh.

### 6. Equipment for Water Supply:

Make sure you've got the means to stay hydrated:

- Personal canteens and water bottles that can be reused again.

- Portable water storage containers are often known as water bladders.

- Make sure your emergency kit includes means of purifying water.

### 7. Methods of Conservation:

- Reduce water waste to increase your available supply.

- Fixtures and appliances that use less water should be used.

- Graywater can be collected and used for non-drinking uses such as flushing toilets or watering plants.

- Share water-saving tips with your family or friends to help everyone save money and water.

### 8. Checking and Repairing:

Maintaining and performing routine water system tests:

- Be sure to check on the water and its storage containers on a regular basis.

- Filtration and purification systems should be checked and serviced as needed.

- Maintain pure, uncontaminated water supplies at all times.

### 9. Contingency Plans:

Prepare for the unexpected:

- If you just use one method to purify water, be sure you have a backup.

- Create back-up water supplies in case your main supply dries up.

### 10. Training and Academic Enrichment:

Make sure everyone in your family or group knows how to react in an emergency involving water:

- Show people how to get clean water using the right means.

- Water-related emergency drills should be conducted regularly.

## Integrating Tactical Approaches for Enhanced Water Security

Having a reliable source of water is essential for both disaster planning and off-the-grid survival. Integrating tactical measures into your water security plan is crucial to ensuring a steady supply of clean water for consumption. These methods are meant to improve your water-gathering, water-storage, and water-purification abilities in a wide range of scenarios. Here are some important strategies to keep in mind:

### 1. Numerous Water Supply Options:

It's not a good idea to count on just one supply of water. Diversify your strategy by finding and using a variety of watering holes, such as:

- Install gutters, downspouts, and water tanks for collecting rainfall to use later.

- Knowing the locations of surface water sources, such as lakes, rivers, and streams, is essential.

- Check for the availability of groundwater sources like wells and springs on your land.
- Clean water should be stored in containers for quick access in case of crises.

## 2. Filtration and purification on the go:

In order to safely drink water from a variety of sources, it is imperative that you have access to portable water filtration and purification equipment. Strategies can consist of:

- The best way to ensure clean drinking water is to invest in a high-quality, portable water filter with the right filtration capacity.
- Bring along some portable cooking equipment, including a stove, in case you need to boil water.
- Chemical Remedy: Be sure to pack any sort of water purification tablets or liquid treatments.
- Portable ultraviolet (UV) purifiers can successfully kill harmful microorganisms.
- Consider a portable desalination unit in case of an emergency and you are located near a saltwater source.

## 3. Tactical storage:

Pick water containers that are tough, lightweight, and long-lasting. Strategies can consist of:

- Containers for water that extend and contract to save space when not in use.
- Bladders for storing water and staying hydrated while on the run.
- Some tactical backpacks have built-in water bottles so you can stay hydrated without taking your bag off.
- Military-grade containers are appropriate for long-term water storage since they are strong, stackable, and have secure lids.

## 4. Chemicals for Water Purification:

Prepare for water disinfection by stockpiling chlorine dioxide, iodine pills, or calcium hypochlorite. These are great to have on hand in case of an emergency, when filtering or boiling might not be an option.

## 5. Practicing Tactics:

Make sure you and your crew have received proper training in locating, purifying, and protecting tactical water supplies. Learn about potential dangers in the water and how to use the gear correctly.

## 6. Precautions for Water Safety:

Protect your water supply and storage facilities by taking the following steps:

- To avoid pollution or theft, outdoor water sources should be fenced off.
- Water supplies should be monitored by placing security cameras or alarms in obvious locations.
- Padlock water storage containers or use other means to keep unauthorized hands out.

**7. Mobile tactics:**

Think about the need for tactical flexibility:

- Portable water containers are light and compact, making them convenient to bring wherever you go.
- If you have access to tactical vehicles, it is imperative that they have the capacity to store water.

**8. Routine Evaluations:**

It is important to check the quality and safety of your water supply and stored water on a regular basis. Maintain a supply of water testing equipment to identify potential hazards.

**9. Contingency Plans:**

Prepare yourself for the possibility that your main supply of water will be interrupted by developing a backup plan. Find backup purifying procedures and discover other sources.

**10. Records:**

Keep meticulous notes on everything from where you got your water to how you treated it to the results of any tests you ran. Having this record-keeping in place is crucial for monitoring water safety over time.

If you incorporate these strategies into your water security plan, you'll be better prepared to protect, cleanse, and store water in a wide range of situations. Key elements of a comprehensive water security policy are tactical diversity, mobility, and security measures. Make sure your strategy is still relevant and up-to-date by reviewing it frequently.

# Real-Life Case Studies

## Learning from Practical Examples of Successful Off-Grid Water Management

Whether you're trying to cut your environmental footprint, live off the grid, or just be more prepared for crises, off-grid water management is an essential skill to have. Successful off-grid water management examples can serve as a great source of both knowledge and motivation. We'll look at various case studies of people, groups, and institutions that have successfully met their water requirements while living off the grid.

### 1. Taos, New Mexico's Earthship Biotecture:

The sustainable dwelling design known as Earthship Biotecture combines off-grid living with advanced water management. The Earthship community in Taos, New Mexico, has proven that human life can be sustained without the use of grid-connected infrastructure. Their water management is based on the following key features:

- The slanted roofs of Earthship dwellings collect rainwater and are directed into underground cisterns for later use.
- Recycling of this "grey" water can be used for things like flushing toilets and watering plants.
- Greywater is further purified by an on-site botanical cell wastewater treatment system before it is used for irrigation.
- Low-flow plumbing fixtures and water-aware lifestyle choices are only two ways the design strives to reduce water consumption and protect natural resources.

### 2. Oracle, Arizona, Biosphere:

Biosphere 2 is a one-of-a-kind laboratory for the study of self-contained ecosystems. Although this isn't a typical household, it does demonstrate some sophisticated forms of "off-grid" water management. What we may learn from Biosphere 2 is that

- The facility uses cutting-edge technology to cleanse and recycle its wastewater for many reuses.
- Biosphere 2 exemplifies how air-water interactions can be optimized in closed environments to sustain water balance.
- Insights regarding large-scale water management in enclosed spaces can be gleaned from the presence of aquatic biomes like the "Ocean" biome.

### 3. The Oglala Lakota Sioux Tribe of South Dakota's Pine Ridge Indian Reservation:

The Oglala Lakota Sioux Tribe of the Pine Ridge Indian Reservation is a model of fortitude and creativity in the face of adversity thanks to their approach to off-grid water management. Examples of what they do:

- The tribe ensures its members have access to potable water by maintaining community wells that are often powered by wind turbines or solar panels.
- To ease the burden on the public water system, some homes collect rainwater for non-drinking purposes.
- Regular water quality monitoring is an important tool for spotting and fixing pollution problems.

- The tribe teaches its members about the importance of water conservation and other environmentally responsible behaviors.

## 4. In the Canadian town of Collingwood, near Blue Mountain:

Blue Mountain Village is a cold-climate ski resort and residential village that practices environmentally responsible water management. Examples of what they do:

- Snowmelt systems prevent the polluting of water supplies by eliminating the need for salt and chemical de-icers by heating sidewalks and roadways.
- The town's landscapes are watered by recycled greywater from local homes and businesses.
- Smart landscaping conserves water by relying on drought-resistant native species.
- Reduced water and power use is achieved through the use of efficient appliances and low-flow plumbing fittings.

## 5. Costa Rica's CRDC (Center for Collaborative and Regenerative Design):

Regenerative agriculture and decentralized water management are exemplified by the CRDC in Costa Rica. Examples of what they do:

- The facility stores water in natural ponds and wetlands and uses them for irrigation, aquaculture, and other purposes.
- Landscape elements such as swales and berms are effective at collecting and holding rainwater, which is then used to replenish groundwater and stop erosion.
- Greywater and blackwater are treated by on-site biofilters to make them safe for irrigation.
- Planting fruit trees and other food plants in your yard might help you save water on watering costs.

## 6. Earthaven Ecovillage, North Carolina; The Sustainable Communities Initiative:

The Sustainable Communities Initiative places special emphasis on off-grid water management at sustainable communities like Earthaven Ecovillage. Examples of what they do:

- Earthaven's residents use a communal well powered by renewable energy sources to supply themselves with potable water.
- Many households now use rainwater for non-drinking purposes, such as watering gardens.
- To guarantee that everyone has access to a sufficient supply of water, a water allocation system has been put in place.
- Water-Efficient Landscaping: Xeriscaping and Permaculture Techniques help to reduce the amount of water used for outdoor purposes.

### 7. The WaterSeerTM System:

WaterSeerTM is a cutting-edge off-grid water management system that uses atmospheric moisture to generate potable water. As a demonstration of the efficacy of technology in off-grid settings, it provides a long-term answer to the problem of water scarcity.

- WaterSeerTM is an air-to-water system that makes use of wind turbines and subsurface condensation chambers to convert atmospheric water vapor into potable H2O.

- The water demands of individuals, families, businesses, and even cities can all be accommodated by this scalable system.

- WaterSeerTM reduces the environmental impact of the water-sourcing process.

### 8. ARTI, India's Institute for Appropriate Rural Technology:

ARTI's mission in India is to provide rural areas with long-lasting and reasonably priced technology. They are doing things like:

- ARTI recommends installing biosand filters in homes to remove harmful bacteria and other contaminants from drinking water.

- The institute instructs people in rural areas on how to collect and store rainwater for later use.

- ARTI promotes citizen participation in water management projects to ensure long-term viability.

## Analyzing Challenges and Solutions in Various Survival Scenarios

Natural disasters, wilderness emergencies, and urban crises are only few of the many possible survival situations. Each has its own set of difficulties that can only be overcome with a tailored approach. In this detailed evaluation, we'll talk about several typical survival situations, the difficulties that come with them, and some ways to improve your odds of making it.

### 1. Hurricanes, Earthquakes, and Floods:

Challenges:

- A lack of safety, nourishment, and hydration.

- Exposure and drinking contaminated water could cause illness or harm.

- Having trouble expressing yourself to rescuers or loved ones.

Solutions:

- Get someplace warm and dry right away.

- Have food and water on hand in case of an emergency.

- Have a well-stocked first-aid kit and familiarity with basic first aid procedures.

- Bring along a water purification tablet or filter.

- Always have access to two-way radios and other means of communication in case of an emergency.

## 2. Surviving in the Wild:

Challenges:

- The effects of being out in the open during a storm.

- Scarce availability of safe drinking water and food.

- Inability to navigate in an unfamiliar environment.

Solutions:

- Construct or locate a safe haven to escape the weather.

- Develop essential skills for surviving in the outdoors, such as fire building, water purification, and signaling.

- Keep basic survival items on hand, such a fire starter, knife, and portable water filter.

- Send out a distress call with a whistle, a mirror, or a signal fire.

- Find a supply of water and food (preferably plants and insects) first.

## 3. Thrive in the City (During Civil Unrest and Power Outages):

Challenges:

- Possibility of disorder, violence, and looting.

- During disruptions, it may be difficult to obtain necessities.

- Fears for one's safety in very populated regions.

Solutions:

- Get together some nonperishable food, water, and medical supplies to keep on hand in case of an emergency at home.

- Create a system of communication and meeting places in case of an emergency in your household.

- Invest in stronger locks, doors, and security systems to keep your home safe.

- Use portable radios and alert systems powered by batteries to stay informed.

- Don't advertise the fact that you're armed and dangerous.

### 4. Maritime Emergency Procedures (Shipwrecks, Capsizing):

Challenges:

- Danger of hypothermia due to exposure to the elements.

- Food and water are in short supply.

- Difficulties finding your way and possible solitude.

Solutions:

- Put on life vests and make rafts out of anything you can find.

- Use lights, mirrors, or a whistle to summon help.

- Stay as motionless as possible in the water to prevent losing heat and energy.

- Find or build a raft to keep you afloat.

- Always have a go bag packed with necessities like water purification tablets in case of an emergency.

### 5. Disease Epidemics and Pandemics:

Challenges:

- Possible spread of disease and infection.

- There is a lack of healthcare services and medical supplies.

- Quarantine or other forms of isolation.

Solutions:

- Make sure to wash your hands often and wear a mask if necessary.

- Put away supplies of food, water, and medicine in case of an emergency.

- Create a room or area in your house to use as a quarantine if necessary.

- Read reputable sources and adhere to recommended health practices.

- Keep your loved ones close and use them as a resource.

### 6. Sustainability and Life Outside the Grid:

Challenges:

- Inadequate availability of common services (such as water, power, and sanitation).

- Needs in terms of food and materials for self-sufficiency.

- Obtaining knowledge of, and getting used to, new technologies.

Solutions:

- Solar panels, rainwater collection, and composting toilets are all good examples of off-grid systems to put money into.

- Grow your own vegetables and raise some animals if you need to.
- Canned goods, home repairs, and other useful skills can be learned.
- Develop a can-do attitude and downsize to a more sustainable way of life.
- Create a strong support system by connecting with people who share your values.

### 7. Collapse of the Financial System and the Economy:

Challenges:

- Income and financial security are lost.
- Less availability of basic services and supplies.
- Civil turmoil and instability may occur.

Solutions:

- Create a safety net of income streams and learn to weather economic storms.
- Cut costs where you can, and only buy what you need.
- Create a savings cushion for when the unexpected happens.
- Get yourself some marketable skills.
- Think about trying bartering or trading with others in your area.

### 8. Extreme climates (deserts, polar regions, tropical rain forests):

Challenges:

- Severe weather conditions and temperature swings.
- Scarce supplies of both water and food.
- Finding your way and staying alive in treacherous environments.

Solutions:

- Protect yourself from the elements by dressing for the occasion.
- Bring along insulated clothes and survival equipment designed for use in the desert.
- Master techniques unique to your area, such as how to get water in a desert.
- Learn about the local flora and fauna to identify edible plants and animals.
- Make use of local maps or a global positioning system to guide your way.

# Chapter 6

# Basic DIY Plumbing Ideas

## Plumbing Essentials for Off-Grid Living

### Basic DIY Plumbing Concepts and Tools

Off-grid dwellers are required to become self-sufficient in a wide variety of spheres, including plumbing, which is just one of those spheres. Whether you're building an off-grid lodge, a tiny home, or a remote retreat, having a rudimentary understanding of plumbing concepts and the appropriate tools are essential for controlling water supply, waste disposal, and overall comfort. We will cover the principles of plumbing, as well as the tools and supplies that are necessary for living off the grid.

**Concepts Necessary for Plumbing:**

Water Supply:

A well, spring, rainwater collection system, or a nearby body of water (river, lake) can all supply people living off the grid with potable water. Make sure your water supply is safe and complies with all applicable laws.

Water Catchment:

Water storage tanks or receptacles will be required for regular use. Choose long-term water storage containers manufactured from materials like food-grade polyethylene or stainless steel.

Plumbing Fixtures:

Acquire familiarity with PEX, PVC, copper, and other commonly used piping and fittings in plumbing systems. Find out how to properly link them by employing techniques like soldering, gluing, and crimping.

Transfer of H2O:

Think ahead about how you'll get water to all of your rooms. Depending on your location and water supply, you may want to think about installing a gravity-fed system, a pump, or both.

Sewage and Drainage:

A wastewater disposal system must be planned. This may consist of a composting toilet, a septic tank and leach field, or some other environmentally friendly design. Verify that it satisfies all applicable laws in the area.

**Instruments Required for Plumbing:**

Wrench for Turning Pipes:

When working with threaded pipes and fittings, a pipe wrench is required for tightening and loosening. It's a good idea to pack both a big and a little one.

Cutter of Pipes:

When cutting pipes, a pipe cutter ensures a clean, exact cut. To cut copper or PEX tubing, use a tubing cutter, and to cut plastic PVC pipe, use a PVC cutter.

Tape for Plumbers:

Teflon tape is used to make a leak-proof seal on threaded connections.

Plunger:

A plunger is an essential appliance for unclogging sinks, tubs, and showers.

Wrench, Adjustable:

In the world of plumbing, an adjustable wrench is indispensable.

Cutter for Tubes:

A tube cutter is useful for cutting copper or PEX pipes precisely to length.

**Benders of Pipes and Tubes:**

A pipe or tube bender is essential if you need to make a bend in a pipe.

# Chapter 7

# Water Sustainability

## The Sustainable Water Paradigm

### Principles of Sustainable Water Practices

The sustainable water paradigm is an innovative approach to water management that prioritizes environmentally friendly and socially just policies and procedures to secure a sustainable water supply for the future. Water shortage, environmental conservation, and the difficulties brought on by a warming planet all necessitate adhering to these principles of sustainable water management. The fundamental tenets of the sustainable water paradigm are as follows:

**1. IWRM, or integrated water resource management:**

Water, ecosystems, and human needs are all intertwined, and IWRM takes this into account. While protecting aquatic ecosystems, it attempts to strike a balance between agricultural, industrial, and municipal water needs.

To ensure that all stakeholders have fair and equal access to water, it is essential to develop and implement comprehensive water management plans that take into account social, economic, and environmental concerns.

### 2. Efficient use of water resources:

Waste prevention and resource conservation both benefit greatly from water efficiency practices. Households, businesses, and farms may all do their part to save water by adopting water-efficient technology, procedures, and policies.

Water-efficient technology and practices, such as low-flow plumbing fittings, rainwater harvesting, and smart irrigation scheduling, should be widely used to encourage responsible water use.

### 3. Agricultural Sustainability:

Water is largely used in agriculture. Maintaining healthy soil and maximizing water efficiency are essential tenets of sustainable agriculture.

Promote environmentally responsible farming practices like precision farming, crop rotation, and growing drought-resistant crops.

### 4. Restoring and preserving ecosystems:

Wetlands, rivers, and woods are all examples of vital ecosystems that help purify water, prevent flooding, and preserve species diversity. Sustainable water management relies on the preservation and restoration of these ecosystems.

Protect and restore watersheds, riparian areas, and natural habitats to improve water quality, reduce flood risk, and sustain aquatic life.

### 5. Controlling Water Quality:

Maintaining high water quality is critical for both human well-being and ecological balance. Maintaining clean and safe water supplies requires the management of pollutants and contaminants at their points of origin.

To protect drinking water supplies, recreational water areas, and aquatic ecosystems, it is essential to have in place rigorous water quality monitoring and treatment procedures.

### 6. Adapting to a Changing Climate:

The supply and quality of water are both threatened by climate change. Adaptive strategies are a key component of sustainable water practices in the face of shifting climate conditions such as shifting precipitation patterns, drought, and rising temperatures.

Establish water systems that can withstand the effects of climate change, diversify water supplies, and use climatic information in water management plans.

## 7. Reusing water from rain and washing machines:

Greywater recycling involves the treatment and reuse of wastewater from sinks, showers, and washing machines for irrigation and toilet flushing, while rainwater collecting is used for non-potable purposes.

To lessen the need for purified water, it is fundamental to encourage the installation of rainwater catchment systems and the reuse of greywater in buildings.

## 8. Education and Information Campaigns:

It is essential to educate the people about the need of water conservation and sustainable practices. Citizens who are well-informed are more likely to engage in water-saving practices and advocate for environmentally responsible legislation.

Educate people on the worth of water, the significance of water conservation, and the best methods for using water sustainably.

## 9. Structures of Law and Government:

The enforcement of water management policies, the regulation of water use, and the resolution of conflicts over water resources all require robust legal and institutional frameworks.

Water allocation, pollution prevention, and environmental protection should all be governed by simple, easily understood legal and regulatory frameworks.

## 10. Cooperation and Involvement of Stakeholders:

In order to manage water in a sustainable manner, collaboration between governments, communities, corporations, and other stakeholders is required. Procedures for making decisions that are open to participation are beneficial to water policy and projects.

Encourage collaborative problem-solving and shared accountability by incorporating all relevant stakeholders in the planning and execution of water management.

The sustainable water paradigm advocates for water management that is both proactive and integrative, with a focus on environmental stewardship, water conservation, and giving universal access to water. Specifically, the sustainable water paradigm advocates for water management that is both proactive and integrated. By adhering to these principles, you will be contributing to the creation of a water future that is more stable and enduring for everyone.

# Practical Approaches to Implementing Eco-Friendly Water Usage

In order to preserve water supplies and lessen damage to the environment, it is crucial to adopt eco-friendly water usage methods. Individuals, communities, and enterprises may all contribute to water sustainability by implementing these measures and reducing their water consumption at the same time. Eco-friendly water usage can be effectively implemented in the following ways:

## 1. Quickly attend to leaks:

One of the simplest and most efficient ways to save water is to fix any leaks in faucets, pipes, or toilets. The water lost from a leaky tap or a running toilet adds up quickly.

Be proactive and swiftly fix any leaks you find. Washers and valves should be replaced if they are worn.

## 2. Put in low-flow plumbing:

Water-saving low-flow faucets, showerheads, and commodes are available without sacrificing convenience or comfort. They can help you save a lot of money on your water bill.

Reduce water usage by installing low-flow fixtures in place of older models. For the greatest possible water savings, seek out goods bearing the WaterSense logo.

## 3. Gather rainwater for later use.

Rooftop rainwater can be collected and used for things like irrigation, vehicle washing, and even toilet flushing with a rainwater harvesting system.

The rainfall from the downspouts should be collected in rain barrels or larger cisterns. Reduce your needs for potable water by using rainfall you've collected for outdoor uses.

## 4. Replace Old Appliances with Newer, More Efficient Models:

Newer types of both washers and dishwashers use significantly less water than their predecessors. Purchasing water-saving appliances is a good long-term investment.

The ENERGY STAR certification suggests water and energy efficiency, so when it's time to replace appliances, look for it.

## 5. Use Water Efficient Irrigation:

Lawns and gardens that are overwatered are a popular yet wasteful practice. If you use efficient methods of irrigation, you can keep your landscape looking great without wasting any water.

Use a programmable irrigation system that can adapt its watering schedule to the weather in your area. To reduce evaporation, water in the morning or evening.

### 6. Repairs to Fixtures and Water Systems:

Fixing leaky faucets, shower heads, and sprinkler systems on a regular basis saves money and keeps water from going to waste.

Maintaining water pressure requires routine cleaning and unclogging of faucets and showerheads. Immediately fix any leaks or broken parts of the irrigation system.

### 7. Native Plants and Xeriscape Gardening:

Xeriscaping is the practice of landscaping with drought-resistant plants and reducing the amount of water-hungry turfgrass. Plants that are native to an area have evolved to thrive in the climate and soil there.

Take remedial measures by switching out water-hungry plants in your landscaping with drought-resistant or indigenous varieties.

### 8. Put in a dual-flush commode:

Dual-flush loos have a weaker flush for liquid waste and a stronger one for solid waste. Each flush uses less water with these toilets.

Selecting a dual-flush toilet during a remodel or replacement can significantly cut down on water use.

### 9. Involve and inform your loved ones:

Better water saving measures may result from simply raising awareness of the issue among household members or roommates.

Make people aware of the importance of conserving water and get them to stop the water when brushing their teeth or take shorter showers.

### 10. Reusing Wastewater (Greywater):

Gather greywater from sources such as sinks, showers, and washers and treat it so it may be used for things like flushing toilets and watering gardens.

If restrictions in your area allow it, set up a greywater recycling system. Avoid potential health problems by ensuring proper care and distribution.

# Chapter 8

# Finding Water

## Mastering the Art of Water Discovery

### Techniques for Locating Water Sources in Wilderness Environments

One of the most important skills to learn before going on a wilderness adventure, whether for hiking, camping, or survival, is how to find and obtain water. It can literally be a matter of life or death if you become lost and don't know where to find water. In this manual, we will examine several methods for locating water sources in the outdoors.

**1. Take a Good Look Around:**

The availability of water sources in the wilderness can be inferred from familiarity with the landscape. Keep an eye out for these natural landmarks:

- Valleys, depressions, and other low-lying locations are good places to look because water naturally flows downhill there.

- Greenery and a wide diversity of plant life are signs of water availability, either in the form of groundwater or surface water.

- Animals' need for water means that following their tracks or looking for other indicators of wildlife can help you locate water.

- Listen for bird sounds and keep an eye on where the birds are flying while your near water.

**2. Stick to Water Flow Diagrams:**

Understanding drainage patterns that water follows might help you locate water sources. Try to find:

- Follow the contours of nearby hills and ridges downwards; this may bring you to a stream or other body of water.

- Streams, rivers, and lakes can be located by tracing watershed borders.

- Wherever two or more smaller streams come together to form a larger one is often a good place to do so.

   **3. Rely on outside signals:**

   Water sources can be located using numerous clues provided by nature:

- See if the earth is muddy or damp. If the ground is wet or muddy, there may be water hidden beneath the surface.

- It's common for vegetation to flourish near water, so seek out any greenery you find.

- Flying insects like mosquitoes and gnats gather around sources of standing water.

- Following animal trails might help you locate a water source, as all animals require hydration.

   **4. Water, Hear It:**

   A telltale clue of local water sources is the sound of running water. In order to boost the volume of this noise:

- Put Your Hands Behind Your EarPutting your hands behind your ear can improve your ability to hear soft sounds.

- If you have a stethoscope or other listening device, use it to listen to sounds below earth.

   **5. Digging for Water:**

   Dig a "seep hole" or a "sand well" if you think there might be water underneath the ground:

- Dig a hole in the sand and water will seep in over time. Then, using a scoop, remove it.

- Dig a hole several feet deep in sand near a dry riverbed or stream and wait for it to fill up with water.

   **6. Gather Dew:**

   Morning dew is a common occurrence on vegetation and other surfaces. Wiping leaves with a cloth or compressing plant matter will collect dew for you.

   **7. A Solar Standstill:**

   Condensation can be collected using a solar still made from a plastic sheet or bag. Remove the rocks from the perimeter of the pit and set the container in the middle. Condensation forms on the plastic and drips into the container as the ground warms in the sun.

   **8. Observe Animal Footprints:**

   Animal tracks can be used to locate water because all living things require it for survival. Follow animal tracks and other indications of nearby wildlife.

**9. Get a map or a GPS:**

It's a good idea to identify water sources on a map or GPS before venturing into the outdoors. If you get lost or run out of water, this can be a lifesaver.

**10. Bring means of purifying and filtering water:**

It's possible that even if you find water, you won't be able to consume it without purification. Always be prepared to make water safe to drink by packing filtration and purification equipment like a portable water filter, UV purifier, or water purification tablets.

## Reading Nature's Signs: Clues to Water Availability

When you're thirsty and lost in the bush, the signs of nature can be a lifesaver. The ability to recognize these signals is crucial for your survival. Some of the most important signs you can look for in nature to determine where water is located are as follows:

**1. The Flora:**

In the presence of water, certain plant species flourish. Try to find:

You may usually find willow trees in or near water. Cattails are a sure sign of a wetland or marshy location. Cottonwood trees are commonly found in wet areas, such as along riverbanks. Reeds and bullrushes are two types of plants that thrive in or close to water.

**2. Insects at Work:**

Because insects can't function without water, tracking their habits can reveal where to find it. The buzzing of mosquitoes is often a good indicator of stagnant water not far away. Ants typically construct their nests near water, and they often line up in neat rows to drink. Insects like bees and wasps frequently visit watering holes to quench their thirst.

**3. Behavior and animal tracks:**

Animals will congregate around water since it is essential to their existence. Try to find:

Tracks leading to a certain region may suggest that animals are using that area to gain access to water. The presence of birdsong or a large number of birds flying in formation over a small area may point to a nearby water source. Water can be located by following the tracks of creatures such as rabbits, raccoons, and deer.

**4. Terrain and scenery:**

Learning the lay of the ground can yield important information:

Water tends to collect in valleys and other low-lying areas because it naturally flows downhill there. If it has rained recently, search for low spots on the ground that could collect water. Larger bodies of water may be located at points where several smaller streams or creeks converge.

### 5. Weather Patterns and Clouds:

Keep an eye on the clouds and the weather:

White, puffy cumulus clouds are a possible weather indicator of the kind of precipitation that can cause natural depressions to become flooded. A warning of coming rain is the behavior of birds, which tend to fly lower and seek shelter just before a downpour.

### 6. Daybreak and Dusk:

Dew forms on grass, leaves, and rocks when temperatures decrease in the morning and evening. This dew can be collected and used as drinking water: Squeeze the dew out of grass, leaves, or pebbles using a cloth or your hand.

### 7. Dampness and moisture:

Aware of the ambient humidity is important:

Damp or moist soil, especially in dry regions, may betray the existence of groundwater. To reach this water, one must dig a hole. Water can be found in wet or damp rocks or the walls of canyons and ravines.

### 8. Track Animal Signs:

Animals often mark their territory with trails that go directly to water:

Water can be found by following deer or other large animal trails downhill. Animals' tiny footprints could point you toward usable water sources.

### 9. Look Out for Plant and Algae Growth:

Algae and luxuriant vegetation are sometimes seen in places with easy access to water. These occurrences indicate persistent wetness:

Stagnant or slow-moving water is ideal for algae growth. Vegetation Seek out patches where the plant life is denser and more towering than in the surrounding surroundings.

### 10. Make Use of a GPS Device or Compass:

It's a good idea to identify water sources on a map or GPS before venturing into the outdoors. If you get lost or run out of water, this can be a lifesaver.

# Conclusion

The search for water is a fundamental, primitive endeavor in the vast, untamed environment. No matter how experienced or inexperienced you are in the outdoors, knowing how to stay hydrated when you're off the grid is critical to your safety and survival. You now have the theoretical background and practical skills to become an expert in water survival in remote and wilderness places, thanks to this thorough instruction. From the basics of water collection to the nuances of water purification and the obstacles provided by water of different quality, we will study all aspects of off-grid hydration as we delve deeper into the complexities of this essential skill.

Water collection knowledge is the cornerstone of off-grid water supply. Survival in the wild often depends on one's skill in locating and utilizing nature's most valuable resource. This book has provided helpful information on how to obtain water from a variety of natural resources, such as rivers, lakes, springs, and even environmental condensation. With this information in hand, you can go through the wilderness without fear, secure in the knowledge that you will be able to find water when you need it most.

But finding water is only the beginning of the adventure. Water filtration techniques are essential in the bush since you can never be sure of the water's purity. We have explored the many ways that water can be cleaned, from physical processes like boiling and filtering to more complex chemical processes. Each circumstance may call for a unique strategy, making familiarity with these strategies and their benefits and drawbacks crucial. It's important to drink clean water, not merely to avoid dehydration, for a number of reasons.

Particularly delicate and delicate to handle are chemical purification processes. This manual has stressed the need for safety measures when using chemicals in the outdoors. Careless handling of these materials can have devastating effects on both your health and the delicate ecosystems you encounter. Hydration outside the grid requires careful environmental management.

The ecological merits of water discovery and conservation in the outdoors have been investigated as part of our investigation on off-grid hydration. Because of the intricate web of relationships among all of the region's living things, it is imperative that we maintain water sustainability while simultaneously protecting the fragile ecological balance. Leave No Trace principles encourage travelers to leave no trace while they explore a wilderness area, protecting it for future visitors.

This guide has given you the tools you need to overcome the obstacles you'll encounter while searching for clean water in the wild. Developing your water survival skills is just the beginning of your trip toward a more sustainable and self-reliant tomorrow, and this guide will serve as your compass and map.

Off-grid hydration is more than just a talent; it's an attitude that needs to be kept in mind when you journey into the woods. It's a pledge to meet the unpredictability of nature with resourcefulness, responsibility, and resilience. It's about learning to work with nature rather than against it in your search for existence.

With the information you've gained from the Off-Grid Hydration Guide, you'll be well-equipped to live independently in the outdoors. This book has been with you every step of the way, from finding water to purifying it, from caring for the environment to relying solely on one's own resources. May these insights serve you well as you continue your trek into the wilderness and pave the way for a more sustainable and harmonious cohabitation with the natural world. You've proven that you can survive in the outdoors while also protecting its natural splendor by becoming an expert in off-grid water purification. You are now ready to face the rigors of the wilderness with confidence and expertise.

Made in the USA
Las Vegas, NV
18 December 2023

83049871R00044